RAISING AN
AMAZING MUSICIAN
YOU, YOUR CHILD
AND MUSIC

First published in 2009 by
ABRSM (Publishing) Ltd, a wholly owned subsidiary of ABRSM
24 Portland Place, London W1B 1LU, United Kingdom

© 2009 by The Associated Board of the Royal Schools of Music

ISBN 978 1 86096 393 3

AB 2934

A CIP catalogue for this book is available from The British Library.

Design and cover by www.9thplanetdesign.com
Typeset by Florence Production Ltd, Stoodleigh, Devon
Printed in England by Halstan & Co. Ltd, Amersham, Bucks.

Original illustrations © Alan Rowe 2009
Cover photograph by stockxpert.com

Photograph of steel-strung guitar taken by Tom Barry, © 2009 Expertlist Ltd
Photograph of ocarina © Ocarina Workshop; reproduced by kind permission of
Ocarina Workshop®, www.ocarina.co.uk
Photograph of organ © John Norman; reproduced by kind permission of
John Norman and Worcester Cathedral
Photograph of tenor horn reproduced by kind permission of
Besson brass instruments, www.besson.com
Photograph of trombone © 2009 by The Associated Board of the Royal Schools of Music
All other photographs in Chapter 5 by Getty Images

The publisher bears no responsibility for the content of third-party internet websites
found using the Internet search terms suggested in this book.

RAISING AN AMAZING MUSICIAN

Raising an Amazing Musician contains everything you need to know about encouraging your child to enjoy music and music-making. It explains how you can give supportive and informed help to your child from early infancy through to advanced music studies and beyond. It will guide you through the crucial problems of choosing an instrument and a teacher, as well as unravelling some of the myths and mysteries surrounding music and music education. If your children are already involved in music, this book will help you to communicate intelligently with them about it and enable them to get the most out of it.

Participating in music-making is one of the great joys of life: providing children with a musical education is one of the most precious gifts a parent can bestow. Yet there can be so many things to consider at each step of the way that it's not unusual to feel a bit overwhelmed from time to time – whether or not you know about music yourself. This book will help you and your child through each stage of musical development. Sympathetic and sensible, it doesn't make unrealistic promises of instant success – but it does provide real, practical, long-term strategies to help you raise an amazing musician.

Using the book

You don't need to be a musician to use and enjoy this book, as it doesn't assume you know a lot about the subject. Musical words and technical terms are explained when they first appear in the text, and also in the 'Useful words' section on page 166. If you come across an idea you don't understand, it may be explained elsewhere in the book – the index on page 179 will help you to track it down. And throughout the book there are cross-references to other chapters to help you navigate through the information. These tell you where to find information related to a particular topic, or if something is followed up in more detail elsewhere.

From time to time in the margins you will find 'webwords', marked ▼▼▼. These are key words or phrases that will help you research a particular topic in more detail on the Internet, and are often related to specific practical issues, such as finding out about music activities in your town or region. When the webwords include words in "inverted commas" you should include the inverted commas when you type them into the search bar of your Internet browser. If a word is preceded by **+**, you should include the plus sign when you enter the search terms. The term **my** in front of a word means you need to enter some information specific to where you live or the instrument that interests you – for example, when you see **mytown**, type the name of your local town or city, or area of city. If there is a town or city of the same name in another country, for example York (UK) and York (Pennsylvania, USA), it might also be useful to indicate which country you are in. Words or phrases following the word **OR**, and extra words and phrases in brackets, can be added to the search bar to help you refine your search or get slightly different results.

You will find that the vast majority of the book is relevant regardless of where in the world you live. In some instances information relates specifically to circumstances in the UK – particularly when the book looks at matters to do with the education system. However even within these sections you will find that situations and issues encountered in the UK are likely to have parallels in your own country, so while the specific details may not be useful, the general advice will be a valuable guide to any parent anywhere.

You don't have to read *Raising an Amazing Musician* from cover to cover all at once. Like a guidebook to a large country, it can be used in many different ways. You can look at a range of options and plan a long journey, or you can read in detail about each stage along the way. So you might use this book to get a sense of how children and young people learn music, and the different ways in which they can enjoy music-making. As your child grows and develops as a musician, different chapters and sections will become useful to you. Dip in and out as necessary. Use it to review what has already been achieved, to understand each stage of development and to plan for a musical future.

Acknowledgements

ABRSM would like to thank each of the following for their contribution to this book:

Project Editor
Anthony Marks

Contributors and consultants
Paul Harris (author), Anthony Marks (author)
Helen Arnold, Joy Austen, Fiona Barry, Peter Batchelar, Peter Bowman, Paul Cameron, Andrew Eales, Mike Hall, Melanie Henry, Julian Hellaby, Richard Hickman, Edward Huws Jones, Carole Jenner-Timms, Brian Ley, Ian Lowes, Jan Miles-Kingston, Chris Morgan, Penny Price-Jones, Ingalo Thomson, Richard Wright, Lilija Zobens

CONTENTS

Chapter 1

WHY SHOULD CHILDREN MAKE MUSIC?

Can you imagine a world without music?

Music is everywhere in our lives. Whether we like it or not, it forms the soundtrack to our existence. Many of us wake up to the sound of music, and there will be countless other occasions during the day when music might excite, soothe, entertain, divert or annoy us. It has the power to inspire, console and challenge us. We sing in the bath; we whistle when we're happy; we use it to cheer ourselves up when we feel miserable.

Music often plays a major part in social, religious and political ceremonies, great and small. It has led armies into battle and sports teams onto the pitch. It is used to sell us everything from airlines to air fresheners. It emerges from every sort of electronic gadget almost continuously. In short, music is a central ingredient of life.

The benefits of music-making

The first answer to the question 'Why should children make music?' is simply that children will want to take part in a form of human expression that surrounds them so completely. Making music brings a deep sense of joy: it adds another dimension to life because it taps into something that is everywhere and experienced by everyone. And the more that children know about music the more rewarding they will find it. Engaging with music wakes our brains up to limitless possibilities. Anyone making music will be physically involved, mentally alert and creatively inspired. This is true the minute that anyone starts to play, sing, dance, or even listen actively.

The more children know about music, the more rewarding they will find it.

Acquiring musical skills can have profound social benefits too. Music is a universal language – it crosses cultural, social and international boundaries. Children who sing or play with others are not just learning technical and musical skills; they are also learning how to cooperate, communicate and negotiate. These social skills are vital in all sorts of contexts – not just musical

– for children and adults alike. All children should therefore be encouraged to make music with others, and the enjoyment that they are likely to find will make the time spent practising very worthwhile indeed. There will be many opportunities for satisfying music-making from the earliest years through to higher education, and beyond.

▼▼▼ WEBWORDS music + education + benefit OR "social benefit"

Other claims for music education

Research has shown that learning to play and read music has substantial educational benefits for children. Because it requires the coordination of physical, intellectual and emotional activity, it can bring improvements to children's schoolwork overall. Other recent research has discovered that learning an instrument actively increases the size of the brain, and fuels brain activity. In fact, education in music has a positive effect on virtually all areas of learning.

Some experts believe that playing or listening to the music of particular composers can improve general intellectual capacity. (In the late 1990s a research team in the USA claimed that the IQ of a group of students increased when they listened to classical music.) Others claim that music can help to cure a range of ailments – from sleeplessness to skin disorders.

▼▼▼ WEBWORDS music + education + IQ + brain

However, these claims have been and remain the subject of considerable controversy within the scientific and educational communities. And whether we believe the claims or not, music must not be seen as a means to an end. It is important for its own sake.

Music education has a positive effect on virtually all areas of learning.

Music and the development of the brain

Despite the controversy surrounding the claims discussed above, it is clear that learning music does aid the development of the brain, and of learning skills, in certain specific ways. Children who from an early age experience plenty of creative activities (anything from singing, dancing, drawing and painting to playing with building bricks or jigsaw puzzles) seem to have certain advantages over children whose lives are empty of such things. Because creative activities – especially musical ones – engage children both mentally and physically, they strengthen the all-important links formed between one part of the brain and another during the crucial period between birth and the age of seven. More passive activities like using a computer or watching television may not stimulate the links as effectively because the child is not required to process and react to information in the same way. It is now thought that these links may begin to wither away if not activated early; although they can be revived later, the process of doing so may be slow and inefficient.

While learning to make music is unlikely to cause children to become better at mathematics, for example, it can strengthen their developing thinking processes as these strong links are formed in the brain. The brain becomes more efficient and flexible in its handling of a broad range of challenges, whether intellectual, practical, social or emotional. Music also develops children's ability simply to connect one thing to the next. This making of connections is central to all learning, to self-knowledge and thus, ultimately, to an enhanced quality of life.

What music education does

All good teaching and learning is based on making connections – being able to see how things fit together. When learning something new, we usually understand it by seeing how it connects with what we already know. As we make more and more of these connections whenever we come across a new fact or idea, our knowledge and skills develop. A particularly 'clever' person is someone who makes these connections quickly, almost instinctively; a particularly 'musical' person is someone who easily makes connections with regard to music. Good music teachers will help their pupils to make these connections, and so encourage them in 'musical thinking'.

Musical thinking is the way in which musicians make intuitive and instinctive links between all the various elements that make up music. When hearing music, musicians respond with understanding and knowledge. They can probably say which instruments are playing, approximately when the music was written, and perhaps who wrote it. They may also be able to recognize complex technical details about the performance or recording, and are likely to have opinions about what they hear.

When musicians read music, they understand many things simultaneously: they hear it internally (like silently reading a book), they process different sounds and rhythms, and they can understand the music's structure and expression. Though more complex, this understanding is broadly similar to the way we might know, say, a cheese and tomato sandwich. The idea needn't be explained to us from scratch each time. We know instantly what a cheese and tomato sandwich is, whether one is in our hand or not. We know what it looks, feels and tastes like, what its different parts are, and in what order they come (bread–cheese–tomato–bread). We can also distinguish between different types of bread or cheese, and may have firmly held opinions about them.

This kind of holistic thinking as regards music can only happen properly when the whole brain is being accessed and when all types of thinking are fully stimulated and linked. For the few who possess a generous number of neural connections and who are naturally musical this will happen very readily; for others – the majority – it takes skilled teaching to enable the pupil to make the necessary mental connections and bring about the development of musical thinking.

Musical education alone will not therefore turn your child into a musical genius – but it can and will enable your child to engage fully with a stimulating, creative and expressive world.

A few words of caution

Embarking on music education for your child will engage you and your child in a variety of decisions. Even early on it requires some commitment from you both, and this will increase if your child shows particular interest or talent. You shouldn't require vast sums of money to provide your child with a good music education, as help may be available through school, the local education authority or charitable trusts, but you will need to invest some effort.

This book aims to help you navigate through every stage of the process and will enable you and your child to get the most out of music. To be involved in a child's music education can be an enriching (if occasionally exhausting) experience and you can be sure that your child will need your help and encouragement at every step of the way. As with so many other aspects of a child's upbringing, you may run into areas of difficulty from time to time, or have to make some serious choices. Again, you will find help with this in the following chapters.

Your child will need your help and encouragement at every step of the way.

It is worth remembering, however, that the principal reason for a music education is to give a child a set of enjoyable skills which – it is to be hoped – will be of lifelong use. If any conflict with your child over learning music begins to outweigh the enjoyment, something is wrong. The process may not always be entirely smooth, but if music lessons become a real battleground it may be that you and your child have different aims and desires. (There is more about this in Chapter 16.) Presuming all goes well, however, your child should grow up able to make and enjoy music in a variety of highly rewarding ways.

Key points

There are many excellent reasons for encouraging your child to make music:

- It is an enjoyable and enriching experience.
- It has a positive impact on a child's social skills and social life.
- It stimulates the brain in unique ways which aid all kinds of thinking and learning.
- It may promote good physical and mental health.

Chapter 2

MUSIC ACTIVITIES FOR THE VERY YOUNG

Music is a central part of children's lives, whether we as adults are aware of it or not. Instinctively, a baby learns very quickly to experiment with the sounds that its voice can make. Many small children, left to their own devices, start to make up short fragments of songs as part of playing, or use toys as instruments to make a variety of noises. These activities appear to develop spontaneously – children do not have to be shown how to do these things. This chapter looks at a number of ways in which you can help to develop these natural musical instincts in your child, whether or not you know much about music yourself.

Listening to music at home

If you want to encourage children to read, you fill your house with books and make reading a normal daily activity. Making music available to children will similarly stimulate their musical interest. Music on the radio or stereo – even if it is merely a background to the rest of the day – will provide entertainment and a listening opportunity for even the smallest children. (This is less true of sound from the television or computer, as the visual element can distract children from listening.) Music in this way becomes a natural part of daily life – but it's also important to make listening to music an activity in itself.

> **It's important to make listening to music an activity in itself – not just an accompaniment to the rest of your day.**

The choice of what to listen to is less crucial than your choosing to listen to something in the first place. Many children enjoy music that is tailor-made for them: nursery-rhyme recordings, for example, have an advantage in that you can sing along. Yet children can develop sophisticated tastes in music early on, so you could try everything that you enjoy listening to yourself, as well as music you aren't familiar with, and watch for a reaction such as focused concentration, following the sound, or moving in time to the music. Very young children tend to respond most noticeably to lively, energetic music with bright sounds and a pronounced beat (much like they prefer bright colours to subtle shades), but slower, quieter music may hold their interest too. Try to decide whether your child is listening alertly to something or simply ignoring it, and see what provokes the most enthusiastic and emotional responses.

Once music is a regular feature of the day, children may begin to react to it in a variety of ways. Many will enjoy dancing or moving to music, or they will sing along – even to tunes they have not heard before. They may ask frequently to listen to music and then do so with surprising focus and attention. Often, children aged two and above will love having their own portable music player (there are a number of robust children's music players on the market). This gives them more control of what they listen to and when. It also brings them into contact with technology as they learn to operate the machine – and can give you a break from having to change the music yourself at regular intervals!

Encourage children to talk to you about the music you listen to together. By doing this, you cause them to think about what they have heard and to react to it; you also help them to find the words to express their reactions. With young children (say two to five years) – and older ones who are new to this – the questions need to be simple and straightforward. Linking music to an activity or mood may be a good place to start, such as 'Was that marching music?' or 'Did that make you feel sleepy?'. Asking 'Did it seem loud?' or 'Was this music going very fast?' may prompt children to listen actively and to try to recall what they have heard, instead of just hearing passively without paying attention.

Encourage your child to talk to you about the music you listen to together.

As your child gets used to this sort of activity, ask more open-ended questions – ones that don't just require a 'yes or no' answer. 'What did it make you feel?' or 'What did it sound like?' can be effective in this respect. Allow plenty of time for a reply to emerge – children take a while to absorb this sort of question, particularly if the idea that music can provoke feelings is new to them. You may want to prompt with questions like 'Was it scary? Funny? Sad?' or 'Was it like a bird? An animal? A machine?'. Ask your child to listen to music and then draw or paint pictures, expressing his or her reactions to it. You could simply have music playing while the child paints; more specifically, you could ask the child to 'paint a picture of this music'.

Occasionally – particularly with older children – you might try to make more unusual connections by asking questions that require different ways of thinking, such as 'What colour was that music?', 'Was that tune tall or small?', or 'Was that piece rough or smooth?'.

The object of these questions and activities is to get children to think about the music to which they are listening and then to process what they hear by explaining or reacting to it. Your child may seem to become caught up in the music, engaging and interacting with great concentration. Even very small children do this, and it can be a sign of an aptitude for music.

Going to concerts

Another way to focus children's listening is to take them to live musical events. Children can find it very inspiring and exciting to witness music being made – seeing an orchestra for the first time, for example, is a richly stimulating visual experience. Many orchestras give children's concerts for which the music is chosen to interest young people and is presented in an imaginative and engaging manner. This is an extremely effective way of introducing your child to the world of concert music. In addition, many orchestras and other types of group have their own educational outreach schemes. The person responsible for music in your child's nursery or school should be able to tell you how to get access to these facilities. The Internet is also likely to be a good source here.

WEBWORDS mytown + "family concerts" OR ▼▼▼
"children's concerts" (+ schools)

As children grow, many will be happy at more conventional concerts, but these last up to two hours and the very young may find it hard to concentrate for this length of time. They may be happier with something that is more visually entertaining – musicals, theatre, opera, ballet or pantomime, for example. And look out for school concerts and performances given by youth orchestras: young people often find it inspiring to watch other young people. Again, after attending a concert you might ask for your child's reactions – unless it's clear that your child just wants to absorb the experience without talking about it. Children's enthusiasm may be blunted if they feel under pressure to react to every single piece of music that they encounter!

Musical games

Playing musical games with your child can be great fun, and it doesn't require any particular musical skill on your part. The games described below will help your young child to become accustomed to musical activity. Most of them need no preparation or planning, though you may prefer to think about them in advance (particularly those which require a few household props).

The first objective is to enjoy the games, for they will amuse young children, often for a surprising amount of time. They will also develop in children a number of important musical skills: the ability to listen attentively; the ability to react (mentally and physically) to what is heard; the ability to imagine sound before they make it; and an awareness of rhythm (patterns of long and short sounds) and pitch (high and low sounds). The games may also reveal particular tastes, aptitudes or preferences, which you can help your child to explore in more depth. (See Chapter 3 for more about this.)

7

Don't worry if these games produce results that don't sound much like music to you – you are bringing your child into contact with the nuts and bolts of music and giving him or her a real head start. Most of the games are starting points, and they will develop in particular ways as you go along, according to what feels comfortable for you and your child. With some of them, your child may catch on instantly; with others you may need to persist a little, showing by example what you mean to happen. Give each one some time – but if a particular game doesn't work for your child it might be best to move on to something else before boredom or frustration sets in. It's also important to encourage your child and praise all attempts at music-making. At this stage there aren't any right or wrong ways – for either you or your child – as long as you are both having fun, making sounds, listening to them and thinking about them.

There aren't any right or wrong ways to play these games as long as both you and your child are having fun.

The games below are listed in order: the ones at the beginning are suitable for the youngest children, while those at the end require rather more developed skills and thought processes. You could work through them progressively as your child grows in age, experience and ability, though bear in mind that older children will continue to enjoy playing the simpler games.

8

Sing songs Singing is the simplest way to begin music games. Use nursery rhymes, lullabies or anything that you feel comfortable singing, and encourage your child to join in. Even children who are too young to talk will probably respond by making singsong sounds. If you don't feel confident singing on your own, there are plenty of recordings of nursery and children's songs. But do make sure that you sing along too. For very small children, it is best to choose two or three short, simple songs and repeat them frequently – this helps children to memorize them. Once your child knows a few songs, try the following (in order of difficulty):

- clapping in time to the music as you sing
- singing the song in different ways – faster or slower; louder or more quietly; in a squeaky voice; in a growly voice
- taking it in turns to sing sections – you sing a line, then your child sings a line (try keeping the clapping going as you do this)

Move to music Whenever possible, encourage children to respond to music by moving or dancing. This is not only good exercise; it also helps them to express their reactions to music in ways other than speaking and develops a sense of rhythm. At first, simply play music and move with your child (babies and toddlers could be carried or supported while you move to the sound). Over time, encourage more independent movement. Later, when your child is two or three years old, you could (in order of difficulty):

- give your child ribbons or scarves to wave in time to the music; this helps them to develop control of their gestures in response to music (and will be of benefit later when learning an instrument)
- ask your child to describe the music with their movements (making smooth movements to smooth music, bumpy movements to bumpy music, and so on)
- bounce a ball together – or play catch – in time to music
- ask your child to sing, clap and move at the same time; this develops coordination

Encourage children to respond to music by moving or dancing.

Musical catch With babies and very young children – say up to two years – the best way to begin is to echo back to them the sounds they make. From time to time, repeat your child's vocal sounds or those made with 'household instruments' – a spoon tapped on a tabletop, for instance. This helps children to understand the idea of repeats and echoes and gets them accustomed to listening attentively. Once your child is used to this, try it in reverse, encouraging your child to respond to you by repeating what you sing. Use fragments of a well-known song or choose a few simple notes of your own. Your child may imitate what you sing, and you can repeat the same notes a few times back and forth between you. (Some children will copy you straightaway and easily; others may take a little more time to get the hang of it.) You will be able gradually to change what you sing and develop a sort of musical conversation.

Repeat the above, but this time, instead of singing, try clapping short patterns. You could also use rattles, squeaky toys, other noisy toys or household instruments for this.

Sing, don't speak In conversation, from time to time try singing rather than speaking. (You can do this while your child is still in the womb, as unborn children hear what is going on around them.) Make singing a normal, everyday activity. Use tunes you already know, or – more interesting – make up your own. Encourage your child to reply in singsong rather than in speech.

Make singing a normal, everyday activity.

Make musical instruments Many household objects produce interesting sounds. Constructing and experimenting with home-made instruments helps children to understand some of the elements of sound, and to acquire some of the control skills necessary for playing a musical instrument. (Under-fives will probably need some adult help and support when making things.) Try using some of the following:

- plastic containers filled with dried beans or rice and shaken (see how the sound changes with different fillings and different quantities of filling)

9

- empty tins beaten with spoons (see how the sound changes with tins of different sizes, and wooden or metal spoons)
- jam jars or mugs tapped with wooden spoons (see how the sound changes when the containers are filled with varying amounts of water)

Encourage children to try different ways of playing – loudly, quietly, gently, fiercely – and to listen to how the sound changes when they play the instrument differently. Try making happy and sad sounds, calm and busy sounds, yellow or red sounds – once your imagination is engaged the possibilities are virtually inexhaustible.

A note of caution here – once young children understand that everyday objects may become instruments, they may decide to experiment regardless of where they are, the value of the object, or whether or not it is breakable or dangerous. If you set aside household items which are 'special' for music use, your child will learn that some things are suitable for this activity and others are not. In this way, you may avoid random 'performances' on supermarket trolleys, priceless antiques or light fittings.

▼▼▼ WEBWORDS "home-made musical instruments"

Sound pictures A young child may like to try painting pictures using sound. As a starting point, use ideas that children encounter elsewhere in daily life or in books – this could be anything from dinosaurs to the sea. Make and use some of the instruments described above, or use a piano or electronic keyboard if you have one. For example, use a drum or an upturned plastic bucket to create the sound of a dinosaur running through the forest, or a shaker filled with gravel to conjure up a seaside scene.

Sound effects Tell a story that's familiar to your child, either made up or from a book, and invent musical sound effects together as you go along using either the voice or some of the instruments described above. Children love stories to be repeated, so you can do this several times, refining the music each time. (On every repetition, encourage the child to remember what sound accompanied each event, so that the sound effects become part of the story and can be made automatically.) Later, try getting children to make up their own stories for which they can provide musical sound effects.

▼▼▼ WEBWORDS "musical games" + children (+ ideas)

10

Music classes for the very young

Young children often receive creative development through music at their playgroups, day nurseries and pre-schools. In addition, there are many specialist music classes available for pre-school children which are aimed at developing a musical sense rather than teaching an instrument. They focus on singing and moving to music, and working with the components of music to develop children's awareness – indeed, some of the games listed above may form part of these classes. One major benefit of this sort of group activity is that it gives children experience – often from a very young age – of making music in the company of others. Classes are well worth considering, especially if your child seems to possess a strong enthusiasm for music: they are a way to give practical, supportive help to your child. Many classes give parents the opportunity to participate too, and it is important to do so if your child is going to get the most out of the experience. Parents who share these early musical experiences with their children usually find them stimulating. Some classes are run by teachers who have particular expertise with this age group; others are organized by specialists involved with specific educational methods.

You will find information about this kind of activity in a variety of places – as ever, the Internet is a good source, and a local music shop or local authority centre may have some details. Some classes require that a child is accompanied by a parent or carer; in other classes this may be optional, and a few prefer that children attend unaccompanied. One way to establish what happens is to go to a class to see – this will also help you decide whether such an activity would be appropriate for your child.

WEBWORDS music + class + children's + mytown ▼▼▼

Key points

There are many reasons to make music with your child at home:

- It is great fun for both of you – you and your child are playing together and there are no 'rights and wrongs'.
- It encourages communication and creativity.
- It stimulates the child's brain and develops important thought processes (see Chapter 1).
- It paves the way for more formal music lessons later.

Chapter 3

HOW DO I KNOW IF MY CHILD IS MUSICAL?

The activities in the previous chapter are chiefly intended to stimulate your child's general interest in music, but they will also give you some insight into how your child responds to musical activity. This chapter, which discusses children's responses to music more fully, will help you to recognize musical ability and aptitude in your child. You can then better judge when and how to proceed to more formal types of music training.

What is being 'musical'?

People respond and relate to music in many different ways. Being musical therefore may take many forms – each as valid as the other. Anyone who responds to music in any way is musical. A real enthusiasm for music may in itself be quite enough to secure years of pleasure through various kinds of musical encounter – listening to, enjoying and engaging with music – without necessarily ever learning to play an instrument.

Anyone who responds to music in any way is musical.

But of course there are more practical ways of being musical. Some people have a particularly 'good ear' – an ability to process and understand music instinctively and accurately. This will sometimes be associated with an innate ability to sing in tune or with having 'absolute pitch' (on hearing a note, knowing its name without any reference to a musical instrument or tuning device). Being musical may also be linked to a verbal ability to describe music in particularly vivid ways. Some people naturally produce a beautiful sound with the voice or on an instrument, or shape a musical phrase instinctively and artistically. Others have a good musical memory and can remember and then reproduce a large amount of music effortlessly. And some – even when very young – will display an urge to invent new music.

While these abilities all spring from a basic interest in music, they are separate skills which develop in different ways in different people, and at different speeds. They will improve as young people study and mature. Ultimately, any accomplished musician will have a number of these skills – but probably in different proportions. For example, a famous songwriter may have only the most basic skills on an instrument, and a professional violinist may have little desire or ability to compose music. In the early stages, good music teaching will develop a broad musicality by showing pupils how all the various elements of music connect. As their personal musical preferences emerge, children may wish to specialize, becoming particularly skilled in one or more of the ways described above.

Can anyone be musical?

Everyone is born with some degree of musical intelligence or ability to understand music. Nature provides the basic ingredients that enable all children to become musicians. These ingredients do of course have to be cultivated by training and experience, in much the same way that a child develops other skills such as walking or talking. Skills in music involve a mixture of physical control and knowing how to listen and process what you hear, and they can all be developed from this basic musical intelligence.

The process of acquiring these skills begins with even the youngest children, and is helped by activities such as those described in Chapter 2. Above all, this development depends on a child's having the opportunity to experience and enjoy music. It can continue, through childhood music lessons, into a lifelong love of music (and, in some cases, into becoming a professional musician). Children who are born into families which already include musicians, or musically aware parents or siblings, are therefore at an advantage. The right conditions are in place because music is already part of the child's earliest environment; it is considered worthwhile, and parents will be prepared to invest both time and money in developing their child's musical interests.

Yet just as children (and adults) can learn to become more musical, they can also learn the opposite – to mistrust or suppress their natural musical intelligence. If adults think of themselves as 'unmusical' or 'tone deaf' this is usually because as children they had no opportunity to develop musically. Without the right encouragement, children learn to be embarrassed about what they perceive to be lack of ability. Research has shown that this lack of self-confidence has a negative physical effect on the vocal cords, which become constricted and harder to control under stress. This may explain why 'unmusical' adults find it hard to sing in tune – which in turn reinforces their impression that they are not musical. They not only lose confidence in what they sing, but also lose confidence in what they hear. As a result they lose the vital link (one which musicians take for granted) between what they hear and their physical ability to reproduce it. While this can be remedied in adults by careful training

Adults who think of themselves as 'unmusical' usually had no opportunity to develop musically as children.

and confidence-building, it is important to prevent this situation by giving your child plenty of encouragement.

Truly unmusical people are very uncommon indeed. There is a rare neurological disorder known as amusia, in which elements of the brain's physiology function poorly, leaving the sufferer unable to distinguish music's component parts. However, most people who think themselves tone deaf will probably find, after some expert help, that this is not the case.

Recognizing and encouraging musicality in your child

The first signs of musical interest and ability can come at any age. Very young children may respond to singing or other music going on around them. They might sing to you or to themselves, or may bang toys to accompany music (often in time to the music). This banging is important for a number of reasons: firstly, it helps children to acquire motor skills; secondly, it makes an important link between movement and sound – this will later be vital whatever instrument they may learn; thirdly, it helps a child to experience the fun and drama of performance. Encourage this and you may be setting in motion a lifetime of music-making. Discourage it and you may already be teaching your child to be afraid of making a noise – not a good idea if you want your child to enjoy music.

14

A child is paying particular attention to music when he or she asks to hear a piece of music many times over (or replays on a music player certain pieces or songs in preference to others). If this happens, you might enquire why – is it a particular sound, a particular instrument, a particular rhythm that appeals? Such information helps you to build up a profile of your child's tastes and may be useful when you come to think about a musical instrument. Other children may recognize (and sing along with) the music from television shows or advertisements; this shows that they are identifying particular sounds, memorizing them and linking them to other ideas. Others may pay special attention to sounds – not just music, but everything going on around them – and reproduce them using the voice. Many children imitate the rhythms of household appliances, or will sing the sound of a bus engine as it rises through the gears. You may be startled by these performances, especially those that occur outside the home, but they are evidence that your child is absorbing sound and learning to imitate it. (If you also copy sounds that you hear, your child will be further encouraged.)

Signs of musical ability can include:
- **banging toys to accompany music**
- **showing a preference for a piece of music**
- **recognizing regularly heard music such as television theme tunes**
- **noticing and reproducing background sounds**
- **talking about music**
- **showing interest in musical instruments**

Other musical activities may demonstrate a particular type of relationship with music. For instance, some children may talk a lot about music and be articulate about their likes and dislikes, describing and remembering what they hear (often for a long time after hearing it). Some children will enjoy recording the sound of their own voice (or that of others) – also the sound from any home-made instruments. They may even make up music to record and play back later. A few others may represent patterns or paintings through sound or song, turning what they see – patterned wallpaper, building blocks, toy cars – into a sort of music notation. This may suggest that the child is already interpreting the world musically – something that many people who write music do almost instinctively. And of course, from about the age of three a child may ask to play a musical instrument, and if this is the case you will need to agree on which one (see Chapters 4 and 5) and find a suitable teacher (see Chapter 6).

WEBWORDS encourage + musical + skills + children ▼▼▼

If, on the other hand, your child doesn't seem outwardly enthused by music, don't give up hope. Some children will be more demonstrative about their skills, likes and dislikes than others. Reluctance to sing and dance when you are around should not be interpreted as a lack of musicality – they may yet be absorbing a great deal of music. Children who don't wish to join in with organized singing, for example, may still be heard singing to themselves.

Being musical is partly about a child's confidence and desire to connect with music – some children are inherently confident whereas others gain confidence as they grow older (indeed, learning music may help develop their confidence).

15

Key points
- All children have musical skills and abilities.
- There are different ways to be musical; rather than asking 'Is my child musical?' ask 'In what way is my child musical?'.
- The rate of a child's musical development depends on the level of encouragement and opportunity.
- Children quickly learn either to enjoy or to fear musical activity.

Chapter 4

CHOOSING A MUSICAL INSTRUMENT

Any child who expresses more than a passing interest in music may benefit from learning a musical instrument. Some children may ask to learn, especially if they have friends who play or if they go to a school where music is considered important. Others, particularly younger children, might not be aware that learning an instrument is an option, but if they exhibit some of the musical tendencies outlined in Chapter 3 it may be appropriate to arrange some more formal lessons for them. This chapter considers the many factors involved in helping your child to choose a suitable instrument.

Remember, too, that your child has an inbuilt instrument – the voice. Children should be encouraged to sing from a very early age, and although few children have formal singing lessons, many young people will enjoy being part of a choir or other singing group; this is an excellent way to begin learning music. In this chapter, therefore, and throughout the rest of the book, the words 'play' and 'instrument' are often interchangeable with 'sing' and 'voice'.

Your child has an inbuilt instrument – the voice.
All children should be encouraged to sing.

Which instrument?

Many children know precisely which instrument they wish to learn – they may like how it looks or sounds, or they may have a friend who plays it. These are perfectly valid factors on which to base a decision, and when children have made up their own minds they are likely to be strongly motivated. However, children rarely understand fully what is involved in learning to play, and there may be reasons why another instrument than the one they have chosen would be more suitable (see 'Factors to consider' below). Each instrument has its own particular challenges. Persistent and confident children will overcome them and continue successfully, but those children for whom the instrument was a bad choice may become frustrated or discouraged. You will need to weigh up the benefits or otherwise of steering a child in the direction of a particular instrument.

As a parent you might well have your own ideas: you may love a particular instrument, or have a friend or relative who plays it. These are likewise valid reasons for making a choice, but you do need to listen to your child too. Useful opinions can be canvassed from other parents – and a music specialist at school, local music teacher or expert in a music shop will be able to advise you on the pros and cons of learning the instrument, and on practicalities such as its cost and maintenance. You may also be influenced by the availability of a suitable teacher in your area. But consider the child first and the instrument second. Children will only make progress on an instrument if they are happy with it and with the music they can make, so take a while to reflect before coming to a decision. It won't be the end of the world if you don't get it right first time, and your child can always change to a different instrument later on. (There is much more about this in Chapter 16.)

Consider the child first and the instrument second.

It will be useful to see and hear musical instruments in action, so you and your child could make a trip to a music shop. Some schools or music centres have open days or 'taster sessions' where you can try instruments and perhaps have a sample lesson. Several pieces of music (such as Prokofiev's *Peter and the Wolf*, *The Carnival of the Animals* by Saint-Saëns and *The Young Person's Guide to the Orchestra* by Britten) highlight particular musical instruments: try to listen to recordings or – better still – attend live performances of these works.

17

Factors to consider

Of the many things to think about when helping your child choose a suitable instrument, some concern your child, some concern you, some concern the instruments themselves, and some are more general practicalities. But all of them have an impact on the success of your choice. This section gives an overview of the general issues, many of which are dealt with more fully in the survey of individual instruments (see Chapter 5). The main factors to consider are:

- the age of your child
- the character of your child
- the kind of music your child wants to play
- the cost
- the practicalities (such as size of the instrument and ease of use)

The age of your child Children develop physically and mentally at very different rates, so it is impossible to recommend precisely when to begin learning a particular instrument. A rough starting age for each instrument is given in Chapter 5, but only a teacher will be able to determine whether your child is ready.

Very young children are limited by what they can hold, control and understand – yet children as young as three can begin the violin, while at five (and sometimes younger) many are ready to begin the piano. These, therefore, are instruments that should be considered if your child is very young and expressing a real desire to play. At this age instrumental lessons can follow on seamlessly from many of the musical experiences described in Chapter 2. Some other instruments may be possible as long as children have the appropriate physique and strength, but some woodwind and brass instruments, for example, have certain physiological requirements such as the size of the jaw and the development of the mouth and teeth. If a qualified teacher advises that your child is not quite ready for the instrument of his or her choice, it is often possible to bridge the gap with another 'preparatory' instrument.

Children as young as three can successfully begin learning a musical instrument.

Plenty of teachers now specialize in working with the very young, particularly on the violin and piano. There are advantages and disadvantages associated with starting younger than average, and the sensitive parent should be aware of them. Music lessons tap in directly to the innate musicality of the very young, and habits and skills are quickly developed while children are at their most receptive (and least self-conscious). Many famous musicians – particularly in the classical field – started at a very tender age. Much recent research has proved (unsurprisingly) that the more you practise the more proficient you become – so, in many ways, the earlier you start the better. But parents need to take care not to force very young children. If a child does show early talent, too much parental pressure may lead to a loss of interest or even burn-out.

Other teachers prefer to take school-age beginners who, because they have already developed reading skills, will find the reading and understanding of musical notation easier. There is no upper age limit for starting an instrument: children of any age (or adults) can start from scratch and, given the right teaching and encouragement, can achieve considerable success. Those who begin in their teenage years, for example, often make rapid progress.

There is no upper age limit for starting an instrument.

The character of your child Some young children will instantly feel comfortable with the process of music lessons – which may entail visiting a teacher outside the home, or taking part in larger groups. More timid children may not feel so comfortable at first, but are likely to develop confidence with the support and guidance of a sympathetic teacher. If your child is very gregarious, he or she may want to learn an instrument that can easily be played with others. Most instruments fit this category, and can be both learned and played in groups. (There is more on group lessons in Chapter 6.) Even very junior players of string and wind instruments can find opportunities to take part in an orchestra or band. Other instruments are rather more solitary. The piano is an obvious example: while it can be successfully taught in group lessons, most children practise and play alone for the majority of the time.

Other aspects of your child's character may affect your decision too. A shy child may get an enormous amount out of lessons in the first instance by learning, playing and exploring the instrument alone. Many such children will soon grow in confidence as a result of their musical achievements and this may have a positive impact on all other aspects of their life. And children with special needs can derive particular benefits from learning certain instruments or from specialist approaches to music teaching. (Chapter 17 deals with this subject in detail.)

The kind of music your child wants to play Your child's liking for a particular type of music may help you in the choice of instrument. For example, a child who sings constantly around the home will probably enjoy singing in a choir; one who responds to recordings of African drumming may well take to percussion. Some instruments are more adaptable than others and can be used in many different musical styles; others function in more specific contexts. Instruments such as piano, electronic keyboard and guitar are very 'self-sufficient'; since they can play several notes at once to provide both melody and accompaniment, solo music-making on these instruments can be very rewarding. Others, such as most wind instruments, play only one note at a time and so tend to be played with other musicians. If your child wishes to play in an orchestra, the flute or the violin (for example) would be more suitable than the guitar or the piano (these are rarely used in orchestras). A child who prefers pop music will probably enjoy learning electric guitar, electronic keyboards or drums. (Each instrument's stylistic and social possibilities are considered in Chapter 5.)

19

> **Some instruments are more adaptable than others and can be used in many different musical styles.**

Bear in mind that children's musical tastes are still at a formative stage and children will often enjoy many different types of music. It is quite common for a child to have a variety of musical ambitions and be equally happy playing the flute in the school orchestra, making up dance routines and songs around an electronic keyboard with a group of friends, and singing in a local choir. Parents should try not to allow their own preferences to restrict their children's choices, since music-making of all kinds will give children pleasure, stimulate their interest, broaden their knowledge and develop their skills.

> **Parents should not allow their own preferences to restrict their children's choices.**

The cost Some instruments will obviously be more expensive than others, but there can be other costs: extra items such as replacement strings or reeds, or software and peripherals for electronic instruments; general maintenance and servicing; or the need for a replacement instrument as children grow in size or a better-quality one as they grow in ability. Chapter 5 looks at this in detail. The way you choose to obtain the instrument will also affect how much you pay (see 'Buy, rent or borrow' below).

The practicalities Large and heavy instruments may be unsuitable simply because they are difficult to carry to and from school, lessons or rehearsals. If you choose to transport the instrument by car, you need to be sure that your vehicle is large enough and that you will have the time to act as a taxi service (for both child and instrument) as and when necessary. Where you live may be a factor here – a child may be discouraged from playing by having to drag a  heavy instrument up to and down from a sixth-floor flat. Consider also whether you have enough space for a large instrument – it will need to be kept in a place where it won't be damaged and where your child can play it as often as possible.

Some instruments make a louder noise than others. This may be an important consideration for you – and for your neighbours. The sound you hear when trying an instrument in a large music shop is very different from the sound heard when your child is practising in the next room. Moreover, it takes longer to master the basics on some instruments than on others, so during the early stages of learning you may need to welcome some rather unusual noises into your home – day after day – while your child acquires the necessary rudimentary skills. Chapter 5 considers all these elements.

Most instruments need to be prepared for playing in some way. This ranges from plugging in and switching on (in the case of electronic keyboards) to fitting the pieces together in the correct order and position (in the case of many wind instruments). While all this is taught in music lessons, consider whether your child has sufficient manual skills to manage a perhaps complex set-up procedure (you won't always be there to help). A child who feels intimidated by this is unlikely to be motivated to pick up the instrument to play. And all instruments need to be looked after carefully to keep them in good condition. The amount of intervention varies, however: some instruments are very robust and will withstand a certain amount of neglect, while others are fragile and sensitive and will require frequent attention. If your child is naturally careful, this is unlikely to be a problem under normal circumstances – but damaged instruments are frustrating to play (if they can be played at all) and can be expensive to fix.

All instruments need to be looked after carefully to keep them in good condition.

Buy, rent or borrow?

You may not wish to buy an instrument immediately in case it turns out not to suit your child. In the UK, some music services (organizations contracted by the local education authority to provide music tuition in state schools and at music centres) and schools offer instruments on loan to beginners; many others (including some retailers) operate rental systems that, for a small fee, provide for an experimental trial period. This is invaluable for the more expensive instruments as it allows your child to get a feel for what is involved in learning, playing and maintaining the instrument before a large sum of money is spent on buying one. With many instruments, however, the cost of renting an instrument for six months may be only marginally cheaper than buying one – this is certainly true of student models for beginners, which are usually perfectly adequate and also inexpensive.

WEBWORDS "musical instrument" + hire OR rental + mytown ▼▼▼

21

The instrument must be appropriate for your child, however you intend to obtain it. Learning on a sub-standard instrument is extremely demoralizing and will prevent your child progressing. You do not have to buy the most expensive instrument, but it must be fit for purpose and properly set up to suit your child – try to consult a teacher or music shop. If you are offered the loan of an instrument by a friend or family member, or are considering purchase of a second-hand instrument, a teacher should check it for suitability before it is used. However good an instrument is, it may not necessarily be appropriate for your child. Most young string players, for example, begin learning on specially made smaller instruments and will find it very uncomfortable – if not impossible – to play an instrument that is too large.

If your child shows real interest in continuing with the instrument, you will probably want to purchase one. There is a psychological benefit here since a child will often take much greater pride in his or her own instrument. A good instrument is great for morale and will undoubtedly aid progress. But instrument purchase can be expensive, so always seek advice from a teacher or other professional before buying. Some instruments (particularly string instruments), if wisely chosen, will generally hold or even increase their value over time. And with many instruments you will usually recoup a good proportion of your original spend if you do have to sell again later.

A child will take much greater pride in his or her own instrument.

Many local education authorities, music services and schools in the UK offer financial assistance to parents who want to buy a musical instrument for their child, and loans may also be available from some arts and charitable organizations, so it is worth researching all of your options before making a purchase.

▼▼▼ WEBWORDS mycounty OR myborough + "music service" + "assisted purchase scheme" OR "instrument loan scheme"

Once an instrument has been purchased, it needs to be properly insured. You may find that your own home contents insurance policy does not provide adequately for the instrument or does not deal specifically with musical instruments. It is usually advisable to insure the instrument separately with a company that specializes in insuring musical instruments – particularly if the instrument is of some value – as this kind of company best understands the sorts of claims that might ensue.

▼▼▼ WEBWORDS "musical instrument" + insurance

Key points

- You or your child may have ideas about which instrument to choose, but always consult a shop, school, music teacher, or other specialist as well.
- There are many different factors to consider when choosing an instrument, so take your time to reach a decision and be sensitive to your child's musical preferences.
- Often you will be able to borrow or rent an instrument for your child to try before making the decision to buy.
- Seek advice from an expert before buying an instrument.
- Make sure that musical instruments are adequately insured.

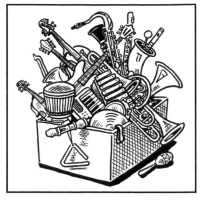

Chapter 5

INSTRUMENT BY
INSTRUMENT

The most common musical instruments are listed in alphabetical order below. The accompanying information is intended to help in identifying suitable instruments for your child, based on the various factors discussed in Chapter 4, and might be a useful starting point. However, before coming to a decision, there is no substitute for talking to specialist teachers or other music experts – as well as to your child. The list includes instruments that may be offered at school, and these are from a variety of cultures and musical styles. It does not include certain traditional instruments that are rarely available to children in school or via mainstream music services; these are usually accessed by individuals within specific communities.

Any instrument name shown in *italic* type has its own entry elsewhere in the list. Some instruments are played in specific types of group or ensemble, and this is mentioned below. For more information about these groups, see 'Types of music-making activity' in Chapter 11.

You can find out more about many of the instruments listed here by visiting ABRSM's SoundJunction website (look for ⟨soundjunction⟩ alongside the instru - ment listing). Visit www.soundjunction.org/amazing.aspa to see and hear instruments being played, listen to interviews with performers, and find out how different instruments work.

Please note that the photographs of the instruments shown in this chapter are not to scale relative to each other. For an indication of the size and manage - ability of an instrument, please refer to its portability rating (see below).

What the numbers and symbols mean

 Minimum starting age
What would be an approximate minimum age at which to start learning the instrument? (Note that in many cases the size and strength of the child may be more relevant than his or her age – ask a specialist for advice.)

 Portability
How easy is it for a child to carry the instrument?
🧳 = small and light
🧳🧳🧳 = bulky, but manageable
🧳🧳🧳🧳🧳 = large and heavy, probably needs transport by car

 Ease of learning in the early stages
How easy is it to learn to play simple tunes and make a good sound relatively quickly?
♪ = easy
♪♪♪ = moderate
♪♪♪♪♪ = difficult

 Assembly and maintenance
How easy is it to put together, take apart and look after the instrument?
✗ = easy
✗✗✗ = moderate
✗✗✗✗✗ = difficult

 Fragility
Is the instrument easily damaged?
♈ = robust
♈♈♈ = reasonably delicate
♈♈♈♈♈ = fragile

 Purchase cost
How costly is it to buy a decent new instrument for a beginner?
£ = inexpensive
£££ = moderate
£££££ = expensive

Running costs
How expensive (in the long term) are repairs and maintenance, replacement parts (reeds, strings etc.) and replacement instruments (larger instruments as children grow, for example)?
➜£ = very inexpensive
➜£££ = moderate
➜£££££ = expensive

24

Adaptability

Can the instrument be used for different styles of music and in different types of group?

Ⓐ = not very adaptable (limited to very specific musical styles and performing groups);

ⒶⒶⒶ = fairly adaptable (might cover a good range of musical styles or a good range of performing groups, but probably not both);

ⒶⒶⒶⒶⒶ = very adaptable (covers all styles of music and a wide range of performing groups)

Moving on

How easy is it to move from learning this instrument to others?

✛ = hard

✛ ✛ ✛ − moderately easy

✛ ✛ ✛ ✛ ✛ = very easy

Disturbance potential

What is the likely potential for disturbance? This is based on two factors: how loud the instrument is, and the kind of sound it makes in the early stages of learning. For those instruments on which it is difficult to make a pleasant sound at first, the disturbance rating should reduce as the student advances.

◀ⁱ⁾ = barely noticeable in the next room

◀ⁱ⁾◀ⁱ⁾◀ⁱ⁾ = may need some negotiation if the neighbours are close by

◀ⁱ⁾◀ⁱ⁾◀ⁱ⁾◀ⁱ⁾◀ⁱ⁾ = impossible to ignore

Bear in mind . . .

This symbol is used where an individual instrument has specific features that may affect your child's choice, or where some particular information is useful for beginners.

25

Accordion
keyboard instrument
7–9 | 🧳🧳🧳 | ♪♪ | ✗✗ | ♈♈♈ | £££ | →£££ |
Ⓐ Ⓐ folk bands and accompanying folk choirs; also used in classical music and jazz | ✢✢ other keyboard instruments | ◀))) ◀)) ◀)) ◀)) |

Acoustic guitar
any guitar that doesn't use electricity or amplification to produce the sound. See *Guitar (classical)* and *Guitar (steel-strung)*

Balafon
an African percussion instrument. See *Percussion (school)*

Bass guitar   🎵 soundjunction
string instrument, plucked
8–9 for safety reasons, child would need to be aware of electricity | 🧳🧳🧳🧳 amplifiers can be heavy and bulky | ♪♪ | ✗✗✗ | ♈♈♈ | £££ | →£££ |
Ⓐ Ⓐ pop, rock and jazz bands | ✢✢✢ *double bass* is the most similar, but also other types of guitar | up to ◀)) ◀)) ◀)) ◀)) ◀)) with amplifier, but can be practised without amplifier or with headphones |
💬 Bass guitar can be less satisfying to play alone, but it is an essential part of many pop and jazz bands.

Bassoon   🎵 soundjunction
woodwind instrument
9–10 needs fairly large hand span | 🧳🧳🧳 |
♪♪♪ quite easy to blow | ✗✗✗ | ♈♈♈ | £££££ |
→£££ | Ⓐ Ⓐ Ⓐ orchestra, wind band, chamber music | ✢✢ | ◀)) ◀)) ◀)) ◀)) | 💬 Some younger players – particularly those with small hands – begin on a smaller version of the instrument. Talk to a teacher.

Batucada instruments
Brazilian drums and percussion used in samba music. See *Percussion (school)*

Cello (full name: Violoncello) ⧉ soundjunction
string instrument, bowed
7–9 | 💼💼💼💼 | ♪♪♪ | ✂✂ | ♈♈♈♈ | £££££ |
➔£££££ a small child needs to begin on a small
instrument, which will have to be replaced as the
individual grows | Ⓐ Ⓐ Ⓐ orchestra, string orchestra,
chamber music | ✛✛ | 🔊)🔊)🔊)

Clarinet ⧉ soundjunction
woodwind instrument
7–9 | 💼 | ♪♪♪ | ✂✂✂ | ♈♈♈ | £££ | ➔£££ |
Ⓐ Ⓐ Ⓐ Ⓐ orchestra, wind band, jazz band, chamber
music | ✛✛✛✛ *saxophone* or ✛✛✛ other woodwind
instruments | 🔊)🔊)🔊)

Clarsach
see *Harp*

Cornet
see *Trumpet*

27

Djembe
an African drum. See *Percussion (school)*

Double bass ⧉ soundjunction
string instrument, bowed or plucked
7–9 | 💼💼💼💼💼 | ♪♪♪ | ✂✂ | ♈♈♈♈ | £££££ |
➔£££££ a small child needs to begin on a small
instrument, which will have to be replaced as the
individual grows | Ⓐ Ⓐ Ⓐ Ⓐ orchestra, string
orchestra, jazz band, wind band, chamber music |
✛✛ *bass guitar* is the most similar | 🔊)🔊) |
💬 Double bass players are always in demand.
Schools are often very keen to start young musicians
on double bass so there may be an instrument
already available.

Drum kit    soundjunction

percussion instrument

8–10 with strength and good physical coordination |
🎒🎒🎒🎒🎒 | ♪ | ✂✂✂✂ | ⚹ | £££ | →££ |
Ⓐ Ⓐ Ⓐ pop, rock and jazz bands and theatre groups |
✛✛ usually other percussion instruments |
◀)) ◀)) ◀)) ◀)) ◀)) practice pads can lower the volume a little |
💬 May be less satisfying to play alone; drums are
usually played in a band. Electronic drum kits are
available (££££) which are portable and can be played
through headphones; however, they will need
amplification for use with other instruments.

Electric guitar

see *Guitar (electric)*

Electronic keyboard

keyboard instrument

5–6 | 🎒🎒🎒 to 🎒🎒🎒🎒 depending on size of
instrument | ♪ | ✂✂ | ⚹⚹ | ££ to ££££ | →££££
instrument will need replacing if the student wishes to
keep up with the latest technology | Ⓐ Ⓐ Ⓐ Ⓐ pop, rock
and jazz bands and accompanying singers or solo
instrumentalists | ✛✛✛✛✛ other keyboard
instruments | up to ◀)) ◀)) ◀)) but can be practised with
headphones | 💬 Keyboards can also be connected to
computers and other electronic equipment. If you are
buying a keyboard to be played like a piano, it is
advisable to look for an instrument that offers 'touch
response'. Also see *Piano*.

Euphonium

brass instrument

9–10 | 🎒🎒🎒 | ♪♪♪ | ✂✂ | ⚹⚹⚹⚹ | ££££ | →£ |
Ⓐ Ⓐ brass band, wind band | ✛✛✛ | ◀)) ◀)) ◀)) ◀))

Flute 🎵 soundjunction
woodwind instrument
7–9 but try an instrument for size | 💼 | ♪♪♪ | ✂✂ |
♟♟♟ | £££ | →££ | Ⓐ Ⓐ Ⓐ Ⓐ orchestra, wind band,
chamber music, jazz band | ✛✛✛ other woodwind
instruments | ◀)) ◀)) | 💬 Young beginners can use a
modified instrument which is easier to hold.

Folk guitar
see *Guitar (steel-strung)*

French horn
see *Horn*

Gamelan
Indonesian percussion instruments. See *Percussion (school)*

Guitar (classical)
string instrument, plucked
6–8 | 💼💼💼 | ♪♪♪ | ✂✂ | ♟♟♟♟ | ££ | →£££ |
Ⓐ Ⓐ guitar ensemble, accompanying singers |
✛✛✛ other types of guitar, particularly *electric guitar* |
◀)) | 💬 Depending on age and size, young players
may need to begin on a small instrument.

Guitar (electric)
string instrument, plucked
8–9 for safety reasons, child would need to be aware of
electricity | 💼💼💼💼 amplifiers can be heavy and bulky |
♪♪ | ✂✂✂ | ♟♟♟ | £££ | →£££ | Ⓐ Ⓐ pop, rock and
jazz bands | ✛✛✛ other types of guitar |
up to ◀)) ◀)) ◀)) ◀)) ◀)) and beyond with amplifier, but can
be practised without amplifier or with headphones |
💬 Electric guitar is a pop and rock instrument first and
foremost, so is most suitable for a child who is interested
in exploring these types of music.

Guitar (electric bass)
see *Bass guitar*

Guitar (steel-strung)

string instrument, plucked

8–9 | 🎒🎒🎒 | ♪♪ | ✂✂ | ⏻⏻⏻⏻ | ££ | →£££ |
Ⓐted Ⓐ guitar ensemble, accompanying singers |
✛✛✛ other types of guitar, particularly *electric guitar* |
◄» | 💬 The steel-strung guitar (also known as folk guitar) is most frequently used in pop, rock and folk music. It is often suited to those who are interested in singing and songwriting.

Harp   ⚡ soundjunction

string instrument, plucked

10–11 | 🎒🎒🎒🎒 or 🎒🎒🎒🎒🎒 depending on size
| ♪♪♪ | ✂✂✂✂ tuning is time-consuming | ⏻⏻⏻⏻ |
£££££ | →££££ a small child needs to begin on a small instrument, which will have to be replaced as the individual grows | Ⓐ Ⓐ folk band, accompanying singers, chamber music, orchestra (occasionally) | ✛✛✛ |
◄»◄» | 💬 Some children begin learning on a small harp, which is easier to transport and less costly. Or children may prefer to learn the traditional harp (or clarsach), which has levers instead of pedals and is also smaller and less expensive.

Horn (or French horn)   ⚡ soundjunction

brass instrument

11–12 | 🎒🎒🎒 | ♪♪♪♪♪ | ✂✂✂ | ⏻⏻⏻⏻ | £££££ |
→£ | Ⓐ Ⓐ Ⓐ orchestra, wind band, chamber music |
✛✛ | ◄»◄»◄» | 💬 Younger beginners often start on the *tenor horn* aged around nine or ten; some manufacturers also make smaller horns that are more suitable for younger players.

Kanjira

an Indian drum. See *Percussion (school)*

Keyboard

see *Electronic keyboard*

Oboe soundjunction

woodwind instrument

9–10 | 💼 | ♪♪♪♪ | ✖✖ | ΥΥΥ | ££££ | →£££ |
Ⓐ Ⓐ Ⓐ orchestra, chamber music, wind band and,
increasingly, jazz | ✢ ✢ ✢ | ◀)) ◀)) ◀)) ◀)) |

Ocarina

woodwind instrument

4 | 💼 | ♪ | ✖ | Υ (plastic instruments) or ΥΥ (ceramic
instruments) | £ | →£ | Ⓐ Ⓐ Ⓐ | ✢ ✢ ✢ ✢ | ◀)) |
💬 The ocarina is popular in schools because it is cheap
and easy to play. It is an ideal first instrument to give
children a taste of music-making, though as with any
other instrument can be played to an advanced level.

Organ (electric)

see *Electronic keyboard*

Organ (pipe)

keyboard instrument

31

The pipe organ is also known as the church organ. It can
be found in places of worship and in concert halls –
home instruments (usually electronic) are available too.
10+ most children begin after learning another keyboard
instrument, but this is not necessary if you can find a
teacher who will take a beginner | 💼 n/a but a pupil
needs to learn to adapt to playing different organs |
♪♪♪ to ♪♪♪♪ | ✖ n/a | Υ | £ n/a instrument would
not normally be purchased by the organist | →£ n/a |
Ⓐ Ⓐ accompanying choirs or congregations |
✢ ✢ ✢ ✢ ✢ other keyboard instruments, but it is more
usual to move from another keyboard instrument to
the organ | ◀)) ◀)) ◀)) ◀)) ◀)) though electronic home
instruments can be played with headphones | 💬 Playing
involves using two or more keyboards played with the
hands, and (for more advanced players) another keyboard
played with the feet, so good coordination and reading
skills are needed. Practising would involve arranging
access to an instrument if you don't have one at home;
costs may be involved.

Percussion (orchestral)

soundjunction

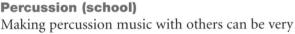

Orchestral percussion instruments include timpani (large drums, also known as kettle drums), snare drum, bass drum, cymbals, triangle, xylophone, glockenspiel, vibraphone, tubular bells, tam-tam, and many hand-held instruments. The orchestral percussionist usually learns to play a large range of instruments.

9–10 with good physical coordination and sense of rhythm | but the percussionist may not be responsible for transport | | | | £ n/a | →£ n/a | ⒶⒶⒶ orchestra, percussion ensemble, marching or military band | can transfer quite easily to other percussion instruments; it is particularly useful for percussionists to learn to play the *piano* or *electronic keyboard* | to |

A set of orchestral percussion instruments might be owned by the school or local music service; practice would therefore usually involve arranging access to the instruments. It is, however, possible to buy practice pads for home use – or to purchase some of the instruments themselves.

Percussion (school)

Making percussion music with others can be very exciting and boosts children's confidence. It often stimulates children to go further – either to become percussionists or to move to other instruments. Many schools and music services give pupils a first taste of music-making using a range of percussion instruments in a variety of styles. These range from equipment specially constructed with young children in mind (Orff Schulwerk, for example) to drums and other instruments from various cultures and traditions around the world: gamelan (Indonesian percussion and drums), samba or batucada instruments (Brazilian drums and percussion), and drums and percussion from Africa (the djembe and balafon) and India (the tabla and kanjira).

Piano
keyboard instrument
5–6 or later as a second instrument for those who have made good progress in singing or on a first instrument | 💼 n/a but a pupil needs to learn to adapt to playing different pianos | ♪ | ✂✂ | ⛨ | £££££ | →£££ | Ⓐ Ⓐ Ⓐ Ⓐ piano duets, accompanying singers or instrumental soloists, jazz band, chamber music – but fewer social opportunities overall | ✢✢✢✢✢ harpsichord or other keyboard instruments, *pipe organ, electronic keyboard* | ◀)) ◀)) ◀)) ◀)) | 💬 As well as the standard upright or grand piano, electronic instruments are available which are usually cheaper (£££), more portable and suitable for the early years of learning; they can be played through headphones.

Recorder
woodwind instrument
5–7 | 💼 | ♪♪ | ✂ | ⛨ | £ | →£ | Ⓐ Ⓐ Ⓐ early music group (playing Renaissance or Baroque music, for example), children's music groups, recorder ensembles, chamber music | ✢✢✢✢✢ an excellent first instrument | ◀)) ◀)) | 💬 There are many types of recorder (listed here in size order from smallest to largest): sopranino, descant (or soprano), treble (or alto), tenor and bass. Children usually begin on the descant. Though the recorder is sometimes thought of as a 'training' instrument, there are many professional recorder players playing in many different styles.

33

Samba instruments
Brazilian drums and percussion. See *Percussion (school)*

Saxophone (alto)   ≋ soundjunction
woodwind instrument
9–10 | 💼💼 | ♪♪♪ | ✂✂✂ | ⛨⛨⛨ | £££ | →£££ | Ⓐ Ⓐ Ⓐ Ⓐ wind band, jazz band, orchestra (occasionally), chamber music, pop music | ✢✢✢✢ other types of saxophone, *clarinet* | ◀)) ◀)) ◀)) ◀)) | 💬 The saxophone can be quite heavy – special harnesses are available to help children to carry the instrument.

Saxophone (tenor)   soundjunction

woodwind instrument

11–12 players may begin on the *alto saxophone*, and change to tenor when they are physically large enough | 💼💼💼 | ♪♪♪ | ✂✂✂ | ♈♈♈ | £££ | →£££ | Ⓐ Ⓐ Ⓐ wind band, jazz band, orchestra (occasionally), chamber music, pop music | ✛✛✛✛ other types of saxophone, *clarinet* | 🔊🔊🔊🔊 | 🗨 The saxophone can be quite heavy – special harnesses are available to help children to carry the instrument.

Singing   soundjunction

0 children should start singing as early as possible, but are usually not physically ready to have solo lessons before the age of eight | 💼 n/a | ♪ | ✂ n/a | ♈♈♈ the voice needs looking after; mild coughs and colds can affect the voice, and smoking (or being in smoky environments) is a disadvantage | £ n/a but as with all instruments, there may be costs involved, such as sheet music, music stand, keyboard and/or recording equipment (for practice purposes) | →£ n/a | Ⓐ Ⓐ Ⓐ Ⓐ Ⓐ choir, bands (pop, rock, jazz, folk etc.), chamber music, opera/theatre groups | ✛ it is particularly useful for singers to learn to play the *piano* or *electronic keyboard* | 🔊🔊 to 🔊🔊🔊🔊 | 🗨 Singing is an excellent way to begin music training because it boosts confidence, teaches children how music works, and encourages social music-making.

Snare drum   soundjunction

percussion instrument

8–10 with good physical coordination and sense of rhythm | 💼💼 but the student may not be responsible for transport | ♪ | ✂✂ | ♈♈ | £ n/a | →£ n/a | Ⓐ military or marching band, brass band | ✛✛ can transfer to other percussion instruments, but would be more difficult to transfer to instruments requiring control of pitch | 🔊🔊🔊🔊 to 🔊🔊🔊🔊🔊 though practice pads are available which are much quieter | 🗨 The snare drum is learned as an individual instrument for the purpose of playing with military bands or marching bands – it is

34

also one of the orchestral percussion instruments (see *Percussion (orchestral)*). Snare drums may be owned by the school, local music service or local military organization; in these cases, practice would involve arranging access to the instrument.

Spanish guitar
another name for the classical guitar. See *Guitar (classical)*

Steel drums
percussion instrument
9–10 I 💼 n/a I ♪♪ I ✂ n/a I ♈ I £ n/a I ➜£ n/a I Ⓐ I
✣✣ other percussion I ◀️)) ◀️)) ◀️)) though rarely used at home I 💬 Steel drums are often taught in schools and community music centres. At first, individual pupils are not usually expected to own, carry or maintain their instruments, but take part in organized classes where the instruments are provided.

35

String bass
see *Double bass*

Tabla
Indian drums. See *Percussion (school)*

Tenor horn
brass instrument
9–10 I 💼💼💼 I ♪♪♪ I ✂✂ I ♈♈♈ I £££ I ➜£ I
ⒶⒶ brass band, wind band I ✣✣✣✣ it is common to start with tenor horn and later change to another brass instrument, such as *trombone, tuba* or *horn* I ◀️)) ◀️)) ◀️))

Trombone
brass instrument
9–10 but try an instrument for size | 💼💼💼 | ♪♪♪♪ |
✗✗✗ | ♈♈♈ | £££ | →£ | Ⓐ Ⓐ Ⓐ Ⓐ orchestra, brass
band, wind band, jazz band | ✦ ✦ ✦ | ◀)) ◀)) ◀)) ◀))

Trumpet
brass instrument
7–9 | 💼 | ♪♪♪ | ✗✗ | ♈♈♈ | £££ | →£ |
Ⓐ Ⓐ Ⓐ Ⓐ orchestra, brass band, wind band, jazz band|
✦ ✦ ✦ | ◀)) ◀)) ◀)) ◀))

Tuba
brass instrument
11–12 most tuba players begin on the *euphonium* or
tenor horn and transfer to the tuba when they are large
enough | 💼💼💼💼💼 | ♪♪♪ | ✗✗ | ♈♈♈♈ | £££££ |
→£ | Ⓐ Ⓐ Ⓐ orchestra, brass band, wind band | ✦ ✦ |
◀)) ◀)) ◀)) ◀))

Ukulele
string instrument, plucked
5–6 | 💼 | ♪ | ✗✗ | ♈♈ | £ | →££ | Ⓐ Ⓐ ukulele
orchestra | ✦ ✦ ✦ *guitar* or other string instruments |
◀)) ◀)) | 💬 The ukulele is popular in some schools; it is
small and inexpensive, and is a good first instrument.

Viola
string instrument, bowed
8–9 many viola players begin on the *violin* and transfer
to the viola when they reach an intermediate standard |
💼💼 | ♪♪♪ | ✗✗ | ♈♈♈ | ££ | →£££ a young
beginner will need to start on a small instrument, which
will have to be replaced as the individual grows |
Ⓐ Ⓐ Ⓐ orchestra, string orchestra, chamber music |
✦ ✦ ✦ usually other string instruments | ◀)) ◀)) ◀))

Violin

string instrument, bowed

3–5 I 💼💼 I ♪♪♪ I ✖✖ I 🍷🍷🍷🍷 I ££ I ➔£££ a young beginner will need to start on a small instrument, which will have to be replaced as the individual grows I Ⓐ Ⓐ Ⓐ Ⓐ orchestra, string orchestra, chamber music, folk band I ✤ ✤ ✤ ✤ usually other string instruments, particularly *viola* I 🔊 🔊 🔊 It can be difficult to make a good sound during the first few weeks, but improvement is usually quick.

Violoncello

see *Cello*

Chapter 6

CHOOSING A TEACHER

The choice of teacher is every bit as important as the choice of instrument, since this is the person who is to guide and encourage your child through all the complexities of music learning. A good teacher will become your child's mentor and friend, and will inspire a lifelong love of music. This chapter looks at the various issues that you need to consider when finding your child's first music teacher.

Why does my child need a teacher?

If an instrument is available, it is likely that your child will want to play it! Many children, left to their own devices, may begin to teach themselves. With some instruments, such as the piano and the recorder, it is possible for a child to pick out simple tunes by ear (hearing notes and reproducing them without using printed music) or simply to enjoy making interesting sounds. Either way it shows that you have a motivated child, so don't discourage this exploration – however noisy it may be.

But a child's desire to make music needs to be carefully nurtured and developed, and the best person to do this is a good teacher. Without one, a child will find it very hard to make constructive progress on an instrument; energy and enthusiasm will quickly turn to frustration and defeat. Although a number of self-taught musicians have become very successful, they commonly express the difficulties that they experienced as children while trying to master music unaided.

Without a teacher, energy and enthusiasm will quickly turn to frustration and defeat.

There are many publications available – books, videos and computer software – which can, if correctly followed, teach the rudiments of playing an instrument and how to read music. These may be suitable for older children and teenagers who show a high level of interest, particularly when, for whatever reason, music lessons are not possible or appropriate. But even the best interactive publications can't give the high level of feedback and encouragement necessary for progress. A teacher can, and is there to act as a constant reference point. He or she will be able to recognize the strengths and weaknesses in a child's playing, and can develop the good aspects and remedy the problems. Learning a musical instrument is a complex process involving precise physical movements and gestures. Only a teacher can properly monitor a pupil's posture and technique; problems in either area, if not caught early, can become serious and even cause the player to give up.

Good teachers will deliver all aspects of musical training simultaneously so that, while learning to play an instrument, children will also develop the rich variety of skills and knowledge needed to become self-motivated and all-round musicians. (There is more about this in Chapter 7.) Finally, a good teacher will be familiar with the wider musical community and therefore aware of all sorts of wide-ranging opportunities for your child to make and enjoy music.

How to find a teacher

If your child is being taught at school, you are unlikely to have much influence over the choice of teacher (indeed, your child's choice of instrument may also be governed by what is available in school; see Chapter 10 for more about this). You can be reassured, however, that the school or local education authority has made the selection of teacher according to various rules and considerations (qualifications, criminal record checks etc.) and that minimum standards have been satisfied. Likewise, if your child is accepted at a specialist music centre or the junior department of a music college, the choice of teacher will very probably be made for you.

Finding a private teacher – one that you select and pay for yourself – can be more of a challenge. Personal recommendation and thorough research are invaluable. Music shops, website lists and libraries are all useful sources for finding music teachers, and the appropriate section of the commercial telephone directory may also help. There are also a number of professional music associations that have lists of teachers; in order to appear on such lists, teachers have to satisfy the association that they are sufficiently qualified and experienced. With some instruments, finding the right teacher may simply be a matter of geography – for example, there may be only one tuba teacher in your part of the country.

WEBWORDS myinstrument + teacher + mytown ▼▼▼

What makes an effective teacher?

Think back to some of your own schoolteachers (in any subject) – especially the ones who made a positive and lasting impression on you. Take a few moments to list the skills that you feel an effective teacher requires. You may be surprised to find the list to be quite long. Your child's instrumental teacher will need many of these general teaching skills in addition to instrumental proficiency and a broad musical knowledge.

Here are some of the more important qualities that you would wish to find in a successful instrumental teacher:

- instrumental skill
- a love and knowledge of music
- communication skills
- personality
- administrative skills
- knowledge of the music world
- qualifications

Instrumental skill A deep knowledge of instrumental technique is essential. However, an ability to play the instrument well is not in itself sufficient: teachers need insight into the process of learning the instrument, and then the ability to express that to others; they also must be able to analyse and correct pupils' technical problems.

An ability to play the instrument well is not in itself sufficient: teachers need other skills too.

A love and knowledge of music Teachers need to care not just about the instrument but also about music and music-making in general. They should have knowledge of a great deal of music and be open-minded about all types and styles.

Communication skills Pupils are individuals; they learn at their own pace and in their own way. The teacher must be sensitive to this and anticipate a variety of responses and reactions. Teachers may have to communicate concepts, skills and abstract ideas in a number of different ways. The challenge for a teacher is to develop a flexible approach which can be modified according to the needs of each pupil.

Personality Enthusiasm, imagination, a methodical mind, a sincere concern for the pupil, a good deal of patience and a sense of humour are all essential qualities. A teacher needs the ability to inspire and encourage – in lessons that are exciting and rewarding. A successful pupil–teacher relationship will create energy and an intense sense of purpose.

Administrative skills Teaching involves many different administrative duties – planning and monitoring pupils' work; organizing lesson timetables; keeping up with payments due for lessons, music and other extras; and dealing with examination or festival documentation.

Knowledge of the music world In addition to their core skills in music and the instrument taught, teachers need to know about the latest music publications; opportunities for music-making outside the lesson (holiday

40

courses, local and national groups or orchestras); music exams and syllabuses; instrument dealers and repairers; and all manner of educational opportunities for young musicians.

Qualifications Teachers may have a university degree in music, or a teaching or performing diploma awarded by a music conservatoire (or conservatory). If the teacher you have in mind advertises 'letters' after his or her name, it might be useful to find out which qualification the letters signify. But some excellent teachers have no formal qualifications – particularly those who have begun teaching after successful careers as performers – so a lack of letters shouldn't necessarily put you off. Some of the world's greatest teachers never took an exam themselves!

Making the right choice for your child

If you are choosing between several different teachers, you need to determine how many of the above qualities the teacher possesses. This may not be easy on the basis of an initial meeting, but it is possible to get an impression of someone's suitability.

You would do well to consider teachers who demonstrate a real interest in their pupils, rather than those who dwell on their own accomplishments. You might ask what books they use to teach music, whether they consider exams important, what styles of music they teach (particularly important if your child has particular tastes and interests), and whether they teach music theory. Teachers who are able to explain to you their methods and expectations (and who don't assume that you will know what they are talking about) are likely to have good communication skills. Ask questions if you don't understand what you are being told, and if you don't find the answers satisfactory, this teacher might have similar difficulties communicating with your child. Teachers who have printed information about their teaching business (such as a leaflet showing teaching periods, rates, contact details and so on) are displaying both communication and administrative skills. And if you ask teachers what opportunities your child might have to make music beyond the lesson, you will find out how knowledgeable they are about local music-making. Above all, you will get an idea of the teacher's personality simply by talking with him or her.

The most important relationship of all is the one between teacher and pupil. Your child will spend a considerable amount of time with his or her teacher and needs to feel at ease. Indeed your opinion is secondary, since children who are happy and comfortable with a teacher will make good progress. A teacher's reputation (however 'good' you are told he or she is) counts for nothing if your child is unhappy, confused or just bored in lessons. It's therefore a very good idea to take your child to meet the prospective teacher, and to see how they get on.

Some teachers are expert communicators with children and will strike up a rapport very quickly. Many are happy to give a sample lesson to see whether the 'chemistry' works. A teacher may want to hear a child sing or play (if appropriate), or observe the potential pupil's reaction to music; the child may also be encouraged to try the instrument for the first time under the teacher's supervision. This gives everyone involved the opportunity to decide whether they think the teaching relationship will work. If you or your child feels that it won't, there is no need to be embarrassed about saying so. Teachers prefer happy, motivated pupils, so it is also in their interests to get it right.

A teacher's reputation counts for nothing if your child is unhappy, confused or just bored in lessons.

You may be able to find out about teachers from their pupils (or their pupils' parents). Some teachers organize end-of-term concerts in which their pupils play to each other and to their parents, and if you are given permission to attend one of these you will be able to hear the sort of work pupils are doing.

Bear in mind, though, that what works for someone else's child may not work for yours. Different approaches – and different personalities – suit different children. A shy child may respond well to an extrovert, demonstrative teacher, or equally well to someone with a gentler, more measured approach. Some children enjoy a relaxed learning environment, while others will flourish with a teacher who makes more obvious demands and operates a fairly formal regime. But all beginners need to feel that they are embarking on a new adventure and that they have a reliable, knowledgeable and sympathetic guide to accompany them.

Once you have made your choice of teacher, it may take a while to establish whether the process is working well. The presence – or absence – of a number of the factors mentioned above may only become apparent after several months. All you can do is keep an eye on the situation. Chapters 7 and 9 will help you to understand the workings of music lessons and how to tell whether your child is making progress. If difficulties arise, you will find a range of problem-solving strategies in Chapter 16.

The practicalities

When choosing a teacher there are a number of practical matters that need to be considered. You will want to ask about the:

- frequency of lessons
- duration of lessons
- venue for lessons
- fees and payment

Frequency of lessons You will need to establish how often the teacher expects your child to have a lesson. The most common approach is one lesson a week during school terms, but this is by no means standard. Some teachers (particularly private ones) feel that a child's progress may be damaged by long gaps between lessons (such as during the summer holidays) so may prefer, for example, a four-term year in which holiday breaks are more frequent but shorter. Some teachers require attendance more or less frequently than once a week. And some may encourage your child to attend additional sessions when music theory is taught, or to make music with other children (see also 'Group lessons' below). Depending on the teacher, these activities may be compulsory.

Duration of lessons The length of the lesson is likely to vary according to the age of the child. The commonly accepted minimum is half an hour, but since young children can find it difficult to concentrate for long periods some teachers feel that shorter lessons are more appropriate. So, for some beginners, lessons may be only 20 minutes. Usually, the older the child is the longer the lesson will be.

Venue for lessons If your child is learning at school or at a music centre, you won't have any influence over the venue but your child will need to get to and from lessons easily (accompanied if necessary). Many private pupils visit their teacher's home for lessons; your child needs to feel comfortable with this, and it should also be practical for you. Some private teachers will visit you at home to give lessons – in which case you must have a suitable room where teacher and pupil will not be interrupted. (You may have to pay more for a lesson in your own home.)

Fees and payment If your child learns in a school or a music centre you are likely to be charged termly, with payment usually due at the start of each term. In the private sector there is variation: you may be asked to pay termly or weekly, for example. Many teachers (or the organizations employing them) will have a formal contract with you which sets out the terms of payment and deals with other issues such as lesson cancellation. It is important to find out and agree what conditions apply if for any reason either you or the teacher wants to stop your child's lessons. The usual notice period is either a term or a half-term.

Group lessons

You most probably imagine an instrumental music lesson as a one-to-one situation in which your child has the teacher's undivided attention. Yet today a good number of teachers prefer to teach children in groups, and indeed many schools and music centres offer only group tuition. While this is partly because of the administrative, practical and financial advantages that group teaching offers, it is also because many people believe that group lessons have particular and significant educational benefits that individual tuition cannot provide.

There are a number of persuasive arguments for group teaching. Firstly, group members learn from each other as well as from the teacher: children find it stimulating to learn by imitating other children around them (the group situation is after all a natural part of a child's everyday routine). Secondly, the learning environment may be less formal and less intense than that of a one-to-one lesson because the teacher has to focus on a number of children rather than just one – and children may enjoy the sociable aspect of being part of a group of musicians. Thirdly, the activities in a group class may be more flexible and more varied simply because a group opens up more possibilities. Finally, many teachers would argue that for some instruments (like percussion) and for some styles of music (like jazz), group lessons are more effective because they develop from the outset the skill of playing with others.

Most groups consist of pupils learning one particular instrument, but groups can also be made up of a range of different ones – a selection of string or wind instruments, for example. In some groups, all the members will be roughly the same standard, while other groups may be mixed ability. A skilled group teacher turns all these different circumstances into advantages – in mixed-ability groups, for example, the more able children benefit from helping the less able, and learn more about their own skills in the process. And playing in a mixed-instrument group encourages children to hear their own part among different instruments. Children who have learned in groups from the outset tend to find little difficulty when they join a band or orchestra because they are so used to group participation.

Some children will benefit from group tuition for many years (group teaching can take pupils to a very advanced level); others, once they are established players, may wish to move to one-to-one lessons for more personal attention and, probably, more intensive study. Many teachers recommend a combination of both approaches to develop all aspects of musical ability – individually taught pupils will certainly benefit from the occasional group lesson.

Advantages of group lessons:
- **group members learn from each other**
- **the learning environment may be less formal**
- **the activities may be more varied**
- **students develop the skill of playing with others**
- **they are often cheaper than one-to-one lessons**

If your child is to have instrumental lessons in school, you may have to choose between group and individual teaching. Both approaches have advantages and disadvantages in educational terms, but before deciding bear in mind also some practical considerations: the time of a group lesson is unlikely to be shifted to suit an individual member, and one-to-one teachers may be more flexible in this respect; on the other hand, group lessons in school tend to be cheaper than one-to-one lessons, whether at school or privately, and might therefore be a more viable option while you determine whether your child enjoys learning the instrument.

Health and safety; child protection

All children have the right to learn in a secure, safe environment, and you will want to feel that any potential teacher can provide this. If your child is taught at school or at a local education authority music centre, steps will be taken in accordance with legislation to ensure that the teaching space is safe and secure, and that the teachers are appropriately trained and qualified to look after young people.

All children have the right to learn in a secure, safe environment.

The situation is less well defined in the private sector. A number of professional organizations insist on establishing their members' credentials before registering them as teachers, so it might be sensible to check whether a potential teacher is affiliated to one of these bodies. Be aware, though, that these organizations cannot monitor every member after registration, and not all teachers belong to these organizations. However, many private teachers also work in local education authority settings and should therefore be approved and registered in that context.

WEBWORDS professional organization + music + teacher + mycountry ▼▼▼

45

However children are taught, it does no harm to reiterate any of the common-sense safety advice you may have given to your child so that, in the extremely unlikely event of any difficulties arising, they will feel encouraged to express any doubts or discomfort they may have. For more information see 'Child protection issues' in Chapter 16.

Key points
- Finding the right teacher for your child is crucial, as this person will be your child's musical guide and inspiration.
- Take time in your research, and try to get personal recommendations.
- Talk to the teacher before you arrange lessons, and don't be afraid to ask questions.
- Try to arrange a trial lesson with the teacher, and listen carefully to your child's reaction.
- Consider the option of group teaching, which many children find very effective.

Chapter 7

WHAT HAPPENS IN MUSIC LESSONS?

Once the selection of instrument and teacher has been made, you can reasonably expect that the excitement and novelty of starting lessons will help to propel your child through any initial anxiety he or she may feel. A good teacher will use this momentum to introduce the pupil to a number of musical activities designed to develop a wide range of skills. Your role as a parent changes. It is now time to watch and wait to see the results, but you continue to have an important part to play in your child's music education: the teacher will be expecting you to support your child's efforts, as you will no doubt wish to do – and you will want to evaluate whether your child is making progress. You therefore need to understand something of the teaching and learning process.

This chapter looks at what takes place in lessons. It isn't a checklist – no two teachers work in the same way, so no two lessons will follow exactly the same pattern – but it will inform you about what a music lesson is likely to involve and the range of skills that your child might acquire.

The first few lessons

Expect the first lessons to be a process of familiarization for all concerned, particularly if your child is starting from scratch and is young. Teacher and pupil will spend a while getting used to each other – and you, too, may need practice in making sure that your child is in the right place at the right time, with everything that he or she needs.

The first lessons will be a process of familiarization for all concerned.

Before lessons start, ask the teacher if you are expected to provide any particular accessories or equipment. Some teachers may wish you to buy a particular music book in advance; others may supply this and charge you for it. You are likely to be asked to supply a notebook in which the teacher can write down practice instructions for your child – and for you.

In addition to a new teacher and probably an unfamiliar environment, your child may take time to be at ease with several aspects of the process – putting the instrument together and taking it apart, learning how to make the first few sounds on the instrument, or beginning to get to grips with music notation. The teacher may wish to enlist your help with certain music activities between lessons, and this will help your child get used to the idea of practising and learning without the teacher. Make sure that you are clear about what may be required. If you don't understand something that the teacher says, do not hesitate to ask for explanation.

Make sure that you are clear about what may be required between lessons.

The aim of music lessons

Before examining the ingredients of a music lesson, it is important to consider what lessons are *for*. The real purpose of lessons is to teach pupils to become musicians in their own right, musically independent of the teacher. This means that, if the teaching has been successful, pupils should be able to:

- play the instrument at the level they require
- understand the components of music and use this understanding creatively
- make informed choices about how to develop their skills in whichever direction they choose
- enjoy lifelong music-making

Good teachers aim to pass on their skills so that their pupils will be able to take ownership of their musical future. In short, they teach to make themselves redundant.

The real purpose of lessons is to teach pupils to become musicians in their own right.

The ingredients of a lesson

Most instrumental or singing lessons will last between 20 minutes and an hour, the duration depending on the age and skill of the pupil, the frequency of lessons, and whether your child is having group or individual lessons.

Whatever the style of music being taught, there are two central disciplines. Firstly, pupils must be taught technique – the physical and mental skills necessary to play their instrument. A teacher needs to make sure, for example, that the pupil holds the instrument correctly, has the correct posture and makes the correct movements. In the process of introducing a basic technique the teacher will usually teach the reading of music notation. Secondly, pupils need to develop their sense of musicianship and artistry – particularly once they have mastered the technical basics. A teacher must therefore be able to help each pupil to interpret music – to communicate something special about it through the medium of musical performance. Technique and musicianship are distinct but closely related, and a well-rounded musician needs both. A good teacher will develop them together.

In order to do this, the teaching needs to include a wide range of activities. These will be taught in different proportions, according to a number of factors. Firstly, the age, ability and requirements of the pupil affect the mix. A second factor is the instrument that is being taught and also the style of music. Thirdly, individual teachers have individual approaches or philosophies – for example, some will teach music notation later than others. But while the balance of these elements may vary, good teachers will expect to cover most of the areas listed below:

- warm-ups
- technical exercises
- repertoire
- sight-reading
- aural awareness
- music theory
- other musicianship skills
- practical skills

Warm-ups These are exercises (with or without the instrument) that prepare the pupil physically and mentally for the rest of the lesson. They are necessary for much the same reasons as they would be for an athlete or dancer: playing or singing demands physical stamina and mental alertness, and it is important that the pupil is adequately prepared. Warm-ups may include breathing exercises, techniques to relax muscles, experiments with posture and holding the instrument, and exercises to encourage the brain to work at its optimum level.

Technical exercises These begin with producing basic sounds and sound patterns through simple routines. A teacher will then develop the pupil's technical skills by means of tone exercises (to develop the sound), scales and arpeggios (chains of notes running up and down in regular rhythm), and studies or more extended exercises (music specially written to develop particular aspects of technique). These will help increase technical fluency and improve the quality of sound the pupil makes. He or she will become able to play increasingly difficult pieces and to play for longer periods of time without discomfort or fatigue – in much the same way as athletes train to develop technique and stamina.

Repertoire For most pupils, learning to play a variety of pieces is the heart of the lesson. In addition to learning the notes, pupils will be encouraged to think about aspects of performance and interpretation (communicating ideas about the music as they play it).

Sight-reading Being able to play or sing music at sight (that is, music that the pupil hasn't seen before) is one of the most fundamental and beneficial of music skills. By including practice of sight-reading in the lesson, the teacher is developing a pupil's ability to turn music notation into sound. In much the same way as reading words gives us access to a huge range of information and entertainment, the reading of music notation allows the world of music to be explored fully.

Aural awareness Hearing and understanding music in your head is very important. Work on developing the musical ear – sometimes called ear-training – is central to good teaching. Teachers will have individual ways of teaching aural awareness, and the 'aural tests' in a grade exam (see Chapter 14) are a small part of this. Imaginative teachers will continually bring aural work into their teaching, through listening, singing, recognition exercises, memory work and improvisation (making up music spontaneously).

Music theory Ideally a teacher will develop pupils' theoretical knowledge in tandem with their practical skills, so that as they learn to play they gradually learn about the 'nuts and bolts' of how music works – the way in which music is written and constructed, its rules and its language, what the signs and symbols mean and how to interpret them.

49

Other musicianship skills Many other musical skills can be developed once the pupil has a good level of technical and theoretical ability. These include composition (writing music for others to play) and improvisation. Although improvisation is particularly important in jazz and pop, it is a very useful skill for all musicians. In a lesson the pupil might improvise in collaboration with the teacher or other players.

A teacher may also want to develop a pupil's ability to play music from memory, or may begin teaching transposition (playing a piece higher or lower than written). Other skills are more specific to particular instruments – guitar and keyboard pupils, for example, may be taught to harmonize (adding an accompaniment part to a tune). All these skills enhance pupils' opportunities to make music and increase their understanding of it.

Practical skills A pupil needs to be taught how to assemble the instrument, how to take it apart, how to put it away safely, and how to look after it. The teacher – at least during the early stages of learning – will deal with aspects of tuning, maintenance, and identifying and remedying problems with the instrument.

'Simultaneous learning'

If you think that the list above looks long and challenging, you are right! Young musicians have a lot to learn, and teachers have a lot to teach them. It is a daunting task to cover all these elements separately in each lesson – especially when each one can be broken down into many smaller items, each of which needs developing alongside the others.

Yet good teachers understand the complex way in which the elements interconnect, and help their pupils to make these connections too. Using a concept known as simultaneous learning, teachers can manage to cover a large number of these areas in a short lesson. They do this by linking each element to the next. For example, a particular piece may be used as the basis for warm-ups, technical exercises, aural awareness and creative work, so that one element of the mix is used to develop a number of others simultaneously. This is more rewarding for the pupil than teaching each element in turn because it is less compartmentalized and better matches the way in which children (and adults) learn new skills and concepts.

At certain times (preparing a piece for an exam, for example) a more compartmentalized way of teaching may be more appropriate – but the pupil will by this time be thinking in a much more musical and confident manner, and this will undoubtedly influence the way a task is approached, both practically and psychologically.

How teachers get the best from their pupils

Good teachers instinctively bring to a lesson the following:

- reassurance
- guidance
- expectation
- motivation

Teachers should always be assessing the degree to which each of these should be applied to an individual pupil, and those who understand and apply the above can reasonably expect their pupils always to try hard and give their best.

Reassurance We are all naturally apprehensive when working with someone who appears to be in authority. A good teacher will overcome that apprehension by creating a friendly atmosphere in which pupil and teacher can work happily together. Pupils must feel confident, comfortable and safe, so a good teacher will reassure pupils by means of constant praise – either unconditional praise (especially for young pupils) or praising as a prelude to positive criticism (for the older ones).

Guidance It is essential that the teaching is methodical, guiding pupils from one musical point to another, making appropriate connections, and making use of suitable and stimulating teaching materials.

Expectation Good teachers always expect the best from their pupils. And because they know each pupil's potential, level of understanding and learning speed, they can set appropriate and reasonable challenges. A pupil is therefore kept inspired to achieve realistic goals without being demoralized by unrealistic demands.

Good teachers always expect the best from their pupils.

Motivation Perhaps the key to maintaining motivation is that the teacher has clear and sensible expectations of the child (see above). Balancing new but realistic challenges with the revisiting and reinforcing of old and previously prepared work should keep up a healthy level of motivation, resulting in continuous achievement.

Curriculum

There are no standard guidelines prescribing the content of private music lessons, so it is very much up to the individual teacher. Many teachers base their own curriculum on moving through a series of graded exams, such as those run by ABRSM (see Chapter 14). Some parents find this useful because it enables them to monitor their children's progress against an external measure of attainment. Many children, too, respond well to these exams because they provide a means of motivation and reward. But while exams are a good measure of achievement, they are not an end in themselves. Teaching which is over-reliant on exams can be limiting unless it is supported by a wide range of other musical activities. Without these, pupils will learn little beyond the exam requirements and the probability is that they will give up – sooner rather than later – with only a handful of pieces in their repertoire to show for their time.

Other teachers will develop their own curriculum based on experience and experimentation, and some may follow teaching programmes based on systems or approaches devised by well-established music educationalists. (Names you may hear in this context are, for example, Dalcroze, Kodály and Suzuki.) Whatever the style or genre of music, as long as a curriculum includes a methodical and progressive approach to technique, a rich variety of repertoire and the development of broad musicianship skills, while supporting musical activities outside the lesson, it can be effective. If your teacher rejects exams altogether, do have the confidence to ask him or her how progress is monitored – there will most likely be a well-considered answer for you.

Many teachers working within a school or local education authority environment, and many private teachers too, use specific vocal and instrumental schemes of work that are closely linked to the school curriculum. Some vocal and instrumental lessons are therefore monitored and assessed using many of the curriculum guidelines.

Contact with the teacher

The contact you have with your child's teacher will be dependent on a number of factors. If the lessons are at school you will meet only occasionally – usually at a school concert or perhaps at an official parents' evening. But most teachers will be happy to discuss with you any concerns you may have – either in person or on the telephone. (Make an appointment first, as teachers can have very busy schedules.) You can also communicate through your child's notebook: the teacher can read your note at the start of the lesson and will respond as appropriate.

Most teachers will be happy to discuss with you any concerns you may have.

If your child is taught privately, there will normally be a few moments of contact before and after each lesson which can be used to discuss general issues. For more serious concerns, it is probably best to give the teacher advance warning so that time can be put aside for discussion. (There is more about this in Chapter 16.) A good teacher will welcome your input, your interest and your questions. Do not hesitate to ask about anything you don't understand – and remember to thank the teacher from time to time!

Remember to thank the teacher from time to time!

Sitting in on lessons

You may want to consider attending a lesson, as this can be a great eye-opener. Knowing what is going on in a lesson will help you to be more supportive over daily practice, and give you understanding of any particular problems and difficulties. (In some teaching methods, like Suzuki, parents must not only attend lessons but also learn the instrument along with their child.) Many private teachers will welcome you into their lessons with enthusiasm, but you should expect to be a silent onlooker unless the teacher wishes to involve you actively in the lesson. If your child learns at school, it may also be possible to attend a lesson, but the head of music should be approached first.

Other teachers may not be so comfortable with a parent sitting in, and you will have to accept their position unquestioningly. Having someone else in the room affects a lesson's whole dynamic, with both pupil and teacher feeling as if they are performing. A young child may feel unsure whom to respond to – their parent or the teacher (who is assuming a parent-like role).

If your child is happy for you to sit in, all well and good – but should your presence stress or inhibit your child, there is little point in pursuing the idea. As children reach adolescence, they often become more self-conscious and may feel distinctly uncomfortable with you there. Adolescent children may use their instrumental teacher as someone to confide in – their lesson may be the only regular occasion when they have the undivided attention of an adult other than a parent, and it may be unwise to disrupt this.

Key points

- Good teachers aim to produce independent musicians with an all-round understanding of all aspects of music.

- A musician needs different types of skill – technical, theoretical and creative – and good teachers use lessons to develop all these elements simultaneously.

- To get the best from their pupils, teachers will provide them with reassurance and guidance, and will have expectations of them that are designed to keep motivation high.

- Teachers use different approaches, depending on their pupils' needs; some will follow specific schemes or syllabuses.

- Take an interest in your child's lessons but be guided by the teacher about the level of your involvement.

Chapter 8

PRACTICE

A good teacher will work hard to keep the pupil enthusiastic by providing a range of activities in the lesson and choosing appropriate music to study. But even the best teacher will struggle to succeed unless a pupil is prepared to devote time and energy outside the lesson as well as in it.

Learning to sing or play an instrument needs practice: the sessions between lessons when pupils make sense of what they have learnt, develop technical skills, and study and repeat pieces until they can play them fluently and musically. As a parent, you can encourage and help with the practising process whether or not you know about music yourself. This chapter looks at ways in which to do this.

You can encourage and help with the practising process whether or not you know about music yourself.

Understanding what practice is

A footballer needs a great variety of skills: physical stamina, technical ability with the ball, knowledge of the game's rules, and an instinct about how to move around the pitch and be in the right place at the right time. Singing or playing an instrument is even more complex. It requires physical strength and the ability to make often very small movements quickly and accurately; it needs an understanding of how the various elements of music connect ('musical thinking'); it must also, of course, communicate the music's character and content effectively.

A good teacher helps a pupil to make progress in all these areas simultan-eously – but they need to be worked on outside the lesson when the teacher isn't there. Normally a teacher will put reminders in the pupil's notebook to help guide and direct practice. A good teacher will also devote part of the lesson to teaching the pupil *how* to practise – showing the pupil ways to make practice productive, interesting, and also fun. If you feel that your child is not being taught this, it would be worth asking the teacher if he or she could spend some time discussing this essential skill.

Football training is not just about playing matches, and music practice is much more than simply playing a piece through from beginning to end. A good practice session may not include any pieces at all. It will, however, include a revision of some of the elements of the lesson. These will depend on the age and stage of the pupil, and the instrument involved, but may well include:

- putting the instrument together (if appropriate), setting it up or preparing it for playing
- warm-ups (including any posture, breathing and relaxation exercises)
- technical exercises (possibly playing the scale and arpeggio of the piece being studied, or inventing or improvising an exercise to help with a technical issue)
- practice of repertoire
- practice of sight-reading
- any or all of the other elements of the lesson listed in Chapter 7
- dismantling the instrument and putting it away

From outside the room, a good practice session might not sound much like music. There may be quiet periods, and not only during warm-ups: many teachers teach the practice technique of playing a piece silently (rehearsing fingering without actually playing) so that the fingers 'remember' movements. Pupils are also taught to read and think music in their heads so that they begin to understand it on a deeper level. (If quiet periods seem very long, however, check that your child hasn't become distracted by some other activity altogether!)

55

A good practice session might not actually sound much like music.

There will also be times where the same few notes are played over and over again as the player tries to make a particular movement automatic. This 'embedding' of movements is an important part of practice. The brain cannot think quickly enough to deal with all the details of playing, so much needs to bypass the conscious brain and become second nature. If a tune, song or other piece is being practised properly, it will stop and start as short sections are replayed (often slowly), fingering or breathing adjusted, and tricky technical issues revisited. Eventually, you may hear the piece from beginning to end.

Not everybody can practise in this way. For beginners in particular, practice is usually based very closely on a piece that is being learned, and a few simple scales and arpeggios. Most beginners understandably find playing pieces more rewarding than any other aspect of practice. But as they become more advanced, pupils should understand the necessity of detailed repetition, of listening carefully, and of using different ways to put problems right. Playing a piece through several times without more detailed work is unlikely to improve technique or eliminate mistakes – in fact, the fingers and body can absorb bad habits and 'learn' to get worse rather than better. If you feel that your child is doing this, it might be time to talk to the teacher.

How to approach practice

A good teacher encourages pupils to develop independent, creative approaches to practice so that they can maximize the benefit. Firstly, pupils must have a clear perception of what they are aiming for – which means that children playing a piece must be able to imagine accurately how it should sound. Familiarity with the desired sound can be achieved by hearing it played by the teacher (or on a recording), or by reading the music and singing the notes, clapping the rhythms or hearing it internally. Secondly, pupils need to be able to hear whether or not what they are playing matches what they are aiming for. If it doesn't, they need to identify why: they may be playing a wrong note, for example, or miscounting a rhythm; the problem may be technical (a particular finger movement or type of breath control may need to be mastered); or it may be about shaping a group of notes accurately. Once a problem is identified the pupil needs to know or devise ways of remedying it – working out what and how to practise in order to make improvements. Effective practice, therefore, involves not only playing, but also listening, thinking, comparing and assessing.

Effective practice involves not only playing, but also listening, thinking, comparing and assessing.

The teacher is likely to have asked for particular aspects to be practised during the week, and to have given ideas on how to resolve particular problems. The pupil may have further ideas of his or her own.

Encouraging practice

Many children find practising unappealing: they often feel that there are more interesting things to do than to stand or sit alone in a room with nothing but a musical instrument and a music book for company. Yet regular practice is essential for sustained and marked progress. Some practice every day, even if just for a few minutes, really will make a difference. There are a few things you can do to help this to happen:

- find a suitable place
- decide on a suitable time
- take an interest
- reward practice

Some practice every day, even if just for a few minutes, really will make a difference.

Find a suitable place Practice needs to take place in a relaxed and comfortable environment where the child will not be interrupted. Children who play portable instruments may like to practise in their bedroom. Drummers and players of electric instruments may prefer to set up in a place where disturbing others is less of an issue (such as the garage or attic), although headphones can be used with some instruments. A piano of course cannot normally be moved, so needs to be practised where it is. Distractions within the room should be reduced during practice time: other family members could go elsewhere, and the television, mobile phone and computer should be turned off. Ideally, noise outside the room should be kept to a minimum, too. The necessary accessories need to be to hand – music, music stand, and any items specific to particular instruments such as a plectrum, drum sticks or reeds.

Decide on a suitable time A routine does make things easier, so encourage your child to practise at the same time each day. Don't hurry or nag your child, but try to make sure that he or she sticks to the same time, unless there is a good reason. Many pupils find that before school is the ideal time to practise, when they are fresh and alert – after school there are the many competing demands of homework, sports, socializing and the need to relax.

How long the practice lasts is another issue. As a rough guide, beginners will practise for about 15 minutes a day; more advanced pupils will need more practice, and an hour a day is not unreasonable. But aim for regularity: a brief session every day is far more useful than a long session twice a week. Ideally pupils should practise for as long as it takes to achieve whatever they set out to do, so try to encourage clear objectives for each practice session and discourage clock-watching!

57

> **A brief session every day is far more useful than a long session twice a week.**

Take an interest Show your child that practice matters. Encouraging your child to talk about it will tell you a little about how things are going; it will also help your child to think about practice as an end in itself (rather than viewing it, as many children do, as time spent 'not doing other things'). Provoking even the briefest conversation about practice shows your child that you know it needs to happen in a particular way. Be prepared to listen and if you don't understand something, ask your child to explain or, better still, demonstrate it on the instrument. If he or she says that something is particularly difficult, try to remember this and ask about it after the next practice session. If it continues to be a problem, it should be brought to the teacher's attention.

Reward practice The most important reward you can give is praise. Tell your child directly – and often – that you are proud of his or her achievement. And, with the child in earshot, tell a friend or relative how well your child is doing. Comments like this really boost a pupil's confidence and self-esteem.

Many parents also give treats to reward children for practising. This may be a good strategy if used wisely. But reward on an irregular basis – if children know that a reward is coming, they will eventually become immune to its effects. It's a good idea to make the treats musical. These might take the form of a recording, some new music, a book about the instrument or small piece of equipment for it, or an outing to a concert or show. If the rewards are always used to encourage children to derive pleasure from music, children will ultimately be motivated by their own music-making. Treats shouldn't become bribes, however, or the child may become more interested in the rewards than the music.

The most important reward you can give is praise.

Sitting in on practice

Beginners especially will benefit enormously from parental help and encouragement with practice and it can be advantageous for a parent to sit in. Older children tend to be more independent and will have less need of (or tolerance for) an adult's presence. (As pupils grow in confidence, they may still like to have a parent in the room while they practise – more for company than intervention. If you sit and read a book while your child practises, he or she may feel less solitary.) Whatever your child's age, if you are to be in the room while your child practises you must both be happy with the idea.

You can help by first looking in your child's notebook to see what the teacher has recommended for practice. If you don't understand what's there, ask for an explanation (this helps your child to absorb the information before expressing it to you) or ask the teacher at the next lesson. Simply go through the list of recommendations, allowing your child to determine exactly what to practise at his or her own pace. Never show signs of annoyance or impatience: to be productive and enjoyable, practice needs to take place in a supportive and relaxed manner. Don't try to teach. You may be tempted to do so, especially if you play yourself or had lessons when younger, but methods have changed and you may end up confusing your child and undermining the teacher. Be careful too about making critical comments – most children expect the teacher alone to do this, and may resent your intervention.

Practice needs to take place in a supportive and relaxed manner.

The content of your child's practice will of course depend on age, level, instrument and teaching method. Here are a few things, however, that you can look out for and try to encourage. If your child isn't doing these things, ask the teacher if they should be included in a practice session.

- Practice should begin with the music book closed. This helps the child listen to the sound and think about playing, rather than looking at the music. After a few warm-ups, some improvising (making up simple music without reading) will get the pupil's musical brain in gear. As well as being creative and encouraging the imagination, this is good for the morale because there are no right or wrong notes.
- If your child is learning scales and arpeggios, they should be played in many different ways – loudly, quietly, using different rhythms, or varying bowing or breathing, for example. (An absolute beginner is unlikely to be doing this.)
- Practice will sometimes include some singing and clapping. Can your child sing parts of the piece? Some teachers – if the instrument is appropriate – may ask children to sing and play tunes at the same time. And can your child clap the rhythm of the piece he or she is playing?
- When practising a piece, a pupil needs to be picking out tricky sections (the teacher will often mark these on the music or in the notebook) and working out how to put them right. This may include repeating finger movements, singing a section to understand what it should sound like, or improvising an exercise to deal with a technical problem.

You may feel that you have neither the time nor the desire to sit in on practice. Your child may also be unhappy with the idea. If this is the case, it isn't vital to be in the room during the practice session so long as, outside it, you are taking an interest in and showing awareness of what is going on. A good teacher and parental encouragement should be enough for most children. (More advice about supporting your child is given in Chapter 9.) But do, from time to time, ask your child to play for you if he or she feels comfortable doing so. And if your child offers to play for you, try very hard to accept, whatever the circumstances. Refusal will deprive the child of one of the greatest pleasures of music-making: the opportunity to perform.

If your child offers to play for you, try very hard to accept, whatever the circumstances.

Key points

- Pupils need to practise regularly in order to get maximum benefit from lessons.
- Encourage your child to make practice part of his or her daily routine; a little practice daily is far more effective than one or two long sessions a week.
- The teacher should advise your child how to practise.
- Practising is much more than playing pieces – it is a creative process that pupils need ultimately to devise for themselves in order to become independent musicians.
- Participate in your child's practice only if your child is happy with this, and do not try to take the teacher's place.

Chapter 9

HOW CAN I HELP MY CHILD'S PROGRESS?

During the first few lessons, most pupils are curious about learning. The instrument and lessons are new and exciting, and this is usually enough to maintain interest in the initial weeks. But gradually children (and their parents) realize that learning an instrument requires commitment and hard work. Because it is a complicated process you may have to deal with various issues along the way, and the way in which pupil, teacher and parent all relate to one another needs thought and care.

This chapter looks at what happens as children learn, how they make progress, and how you can help your child to get maximum benefit and enjoyment from music lessons. For more information on progress, and particularly on how to solve problems, see Chapter 16.

Is my child making progress?

It is natural to ask this simple question, even early on – but the answers are far from simple. There are many things to bear in mind: firstly, children learn at different rates and have different skills and abilities; secondly, some instruments take longer to master than others; thirdly, learning any instrument takes a long time, so swift results cannot be expected. In many ways it is wiser to ask a number of separate questions:

- Is my child happy learning?
- Is the teacher satisfied with my child's progress?
- How do I measure progress?
- What are my expectations from music lessons?
- Is my child making music outside the lesson?

Is my child happy learning? This is the vital question. Does your child go to lessons happily? Do teacher and pupil seem to enjoy themselves during lessons? Does your child practise fairly willingly? Does your child talk about music a lot? If the answer to these questions is 'yes' then the basic conditions for good learning are in place. If your child appears anxious about lessons, you cannot expect quick progress, and if this is the case, you may need to investigate why. (See Chapter 16 for more about this.)

Is the teacher satisfied with my child's progress? The teacher is normally the best judge of how well your child is doing. A good teacher will be continually assessing pupils' needs, progress and achievements and will direct lessons (and advise about practice) in ways that will help pupils to develop at an appropriate pace. Experienced teachers will try to find the right balance for each pupil between challenge and consolidation.

The teacher is normally the best judge of how well your child is doing.

A teacher also understands each pupil's strengths and weaknesses. For example, a child may have difficulty mastering an instrument's technical aspects but be musically able in other ways. The teacher will therefore concentrate on elements that need particular attention while trying to develop all aspects of the child's musical learning. (If this doesn't work, a teacher may recommend other ways of pursuing music that use the child's skills more effectively.)

Do not hesitate to ask the teacher about your child's progress. If there are issues that need addressing, a teacher may prefer not to discuss them in the child's presence, and will arrange to speak with you privately.

How do I measure progress? Parents will be happy that their children are making music and enjoying learning a new skill – but you will no doubt want to feel that your child is making progress too. Given that there are many different aspects of learning music, progress can't be measured simply as a straight line. If your child moves swiftly from Stage 1 to Stage 2 in a tutor book, for example, you may assume that he or she is progressing. But important musical progress can be made by exploring connected topics that a tutor book may not cover, and imaginative teachers may lead their pupils down all sorts of interesting paths before Stage 2 is reached. The result is often a broader music education, and this kind of work often has a real impact on the pupil's later musical growth.

Progress can't be measured simply as a straight line.

From time to time it can be useful to have some form of independent assessment of your child's skills and level of attainment. Graded music exams are the most common way of doing this. These are nationally (and in some cases internationally) recognized tests that represent levels of achievement. Chapter 13 looks in detail at music exams and considers how they can best be integrated into the learning process. Other forms of assessment might be ABRSM's Music Medals (available in the UK and geared towards children learning in groups) or taking part in a competition or festival (see Chapter 15).

There are other ways of judging progress which are independent of exams but have real significance in a child's musical life. The first time a child takes part in a concert will be an important event, for example; another marker of progress is when a song or piece is learnt at home without the teacher's help – this tells you that your child is becoming musically independent. Some teachers, particularly in a group situation, encourage pupils to teach songs, pieces or techniques to those who are less advanced. Such pupils have absorbed what they have been taught well enough to begin to teach it to others.

But progress isn't just about tangible achievement: one of the chief aims of music lessons is to enable pupils to enjoy making music for its own sake. A child who has little interest or involvement in his or her music may still be able to play pieces well. But another who is less skilled technically though far more enthusiastic, and therefore involved in lots of musical activity, is actually making better progress towards becoming an independent musician.

What are my expectations from music lessons? As a parent it is natural that you will have some expectations arising from your child's music lessons. However, these expectations must be realistic. Your child may wish to play a certain tune, or join a particular band or ensemble, or you may wish him or her to sit a music exam. But meeting these expectations will depend on your child's stage of development, and may not yet be possible – for a variety of musical or technical reasons. The teacher should explain to you and your child what needs to happen before a particular goal can be reached, and when you might reasonably expect this to be. Be careful, though, that goals and targets don't begin to take the place of musical enjoyment.

63

Be careful that goals and targets don't begin
to take the place of musical enjoyment.

Is my child making music outside the lesson? One of the best ways of measuring a young musician's development is to look at the amount of music that he or she is making outside the lesson (preferably in as many different settings and with as many other people as possible) and the amount of enjoyment that is being had from it. This enthusiasm does not come from nowhere – it needs to have been generated and then maintained by skilled teachers and committed parents.

Encouraging your child

Encouragement and praise are the two most important things you can give to your child. This is especially true at first, when young children will need to feel that their efforts are being recognized and enjoyed – but even older children who are more experienced and confident in their own abilities need to hear positive reactions on a regular basis. In addition you can help to maintain your child's motivation in the following practical ways:

- keep the instrument in good condition
- reduce practical stresses
- encourage music-making activities outside the lesson

Keep the instrument in good condition It is essential that your child's instrument is kept in good condition. An instrument that is damaged or poorly set up may cause a variety of problems. Firstly, it may be more difficult to play, needing greater physical effort to produce a sound (and making it hard to produce an attractive sound). Secondly, serious physical problems may result if the player is forced to hold the instrument awkwardly or adopt an inappropriate way of standing or sitting. Thirdly, if the instrument is badly out of tune, or hard to play in tune, the pupil will find it impossible to develop a good 'ear' and sense of intonation (that is, what is in tune and what is not). Any of these problems will make learning more difficult and less enjoyable.

Teachers usually keep an eye on the instrument during lessons, and should alert you to any problems. Watch out for signs of discomfort or awkwardness when your child plays, and pay particular attention if he or she complains of pains, strains or stresses. Check that you are aware of any instructions that the teacher may have given regarding regular cleaning or maintenance that your child should carry out. Woodwind instruments, for example, will need cleaning after each practice session to remove any excess moisture. With the piano, unless your child is taught in your home, the teacher will not know the state of your instrument, so you will need to make sure that someone checks it regularly. A reputable piano tuner should visit approximately every six months (piano tuners are listed in directories, though personal recommendation is ideal).

Showing concern for your child's instrument gives out the important message that you value it and your child's relationship with it. A well-maintained instrument is something of which to be proud. Most instruments will benefit from being professionally serviced, cleaned and regulated at least once a year. For woodwind instruments this is essential: other instruments, such as strings, may need more frequent though less serious intervention from the teacher. (Many good instrument technicians work in partnership with specialist dealers, but again there is nothing like personal recommendation.) Electric and electronic keyboard instruments usually need very little attention, except for a regular safety check.

Showing concern for your child's instrument gives out the important message that you value it and your child's relationship with it.

▼▼▼ WEBWORDS "musical instrument" + maintenance OR repair + mytown

Reduce practical stresses Pupils learn best when they are calm and relaxed. If there are practical difficulties regarding their lessons or other music activities – such as arriving on time, and with the right equipment and music – the stress that pupils feel will make them less receptive to the experience. Make sure that your child is well prepared and clear about the arrangements. Plan your route carefully, and allow plenty of time for your child to arrive fresh and unruffled. And if you are meeting your child at the end of the lesson, he or she – especially if young – needs to be certain that you will be there; any anxiety here can distract the child from paying attention during the lesson. Once you have established a routine, try not to alter it without careful explanation to your child first.

Pupils learn best when they are calm and relaxed.

Other stresses can arise at home. The need for a suitable practice space has already been outlined (see Chapter 8), but the realities of finding a suitable time and place may cause conflict with other family members. If two siblings are competing for time at the piano, for example, the enjoyment of playing will be replaced by the stress of disagreement. If a child wants to practise while somebody else needs to work on the computer in the same room, arguments may arise. Again, it helps to establish and maintain a routine.

Encourage music-making activities outside the lesson Music should never be something that only happens in the lesson and during practice. If music becomes part of children's daily life, the chances of making rapid progress are significantly enhanced. Encourage anything that reinforces the idea of music as a means of enjoyment, of fun, of socializing. There is much more about this in Chapter 11, but here is a brief summary of the things to consider:

- Find opportunities for your child to make music with others (your child's teacher may organize group lessons and other activities or know of those who do).
- Encourage your child's less formal music-making with friends.
- Find opportunities for your child to perform – a group of friends could organize an informal concert or play at a party, for example.
- Take your child to concerts and other live music events.
- Consider a holiday music course for your child; children can make tremendous progress on a week's course.

Key points
- When considering progress, remember that children learn at different rates and have different skills and abilities.
- If your child enjoys lessons and practising, and the teacher is satisfied, there is little to worry about.
- Giving praise and encouragement is the best way to help your child make progress.
- The more music your child is making, in whatever setting, the better.

Chapter 10

MUSIC IN SCHOOL

For many children, school is the centre of their musical life. Schools often have very vibrant musical cultures and offer a wide range of music-making, from instrumental lessons to choirs, orchestras, bands, and other groups and ensembles. These readily available opportunities can have a profound positive impact on the lives of young people. Music features in the classroom too – in the UK, music is a compulsory part of the school curriculum for pupils up to the age of 14, so under normal circumstances any child will have a school music lesson at least once a week. Beyond this age, music is optional as an examination subject.

This chapter looks at how you can help your child to get the most out of music at school. It also considers the relationship between classroom music in school and music elsewhere in a child's life.

Music-making in school

School is where most children will have their vital first experiences of making music with other people. Even small primary schools offer pupils the chance to take part in choirs, instrumental groups and bands, and when children reach secondary school they will be able to take part in all manner of music activities in many different styles.

Most schools organize concerts, shows and other events which give pupils the excitement and satisfaction of performing in public, as well as giving parents an opportunity to see the talent and accomplishments of children in the school. Your child's vocal or instrumental skills are likely to be very welcome for events like this, and your child may become much in demand. This can have a very positive effect on pupils' self-esteem, and the more music they make, of whatever kind, the more skills they acquire.

The more music children make, of whatever kind, the more skills they acquire.

Many children are keen to participate in school music but others may be more reluctant: they may be anxious about performing in front of their friends, about remaining at school after lesson time, or about taking their instrument to and from school (an instrument case can make pupils feel different when they are often desperate to conform). And some children simply prefer to keep their music-making separate from school.

Children who start instrumental lessons early, or who attend music classes for the very young (see Chapter 2), will already be familiar with a number of the activities that feature in school music in the early years. They may also understand the fundamentals of music better than their peers. And the benefits go both ways: in school, children will acquire skills – technological ones, for example – that they might like to use in their instrumental lessons.

What happens in classroom music lessons?

Classroom music lessons are for all children, not just for those who learn an instrument. They introduce important aspects of music (how sounds are made and organized, and how music is used for self-expression and creativity) and outline its history and culture. Lessons are likely to include listening, singing, playing and creating music, and will often make use of computers and associated technology. Classroom music teachers also use instruments like percussion, keyboards, recorders and guitars so that all children can have a taste of playing an instrument. The emphasis is on helping children to enjoy and understand music, and to express themselves creatively through making music. School music also encourages more general skills such as concentration, self-discipline and teamwork.

This broad musical education, as well as being important for its own sake, forms an effective backdrop for instrumental lessons (whether taken in school or elsewhere). Children's instrumental skills are enhanced by a better understanding of music theory, history and culture. As their playing develops, children need a wider knowledge of many kinds of music, which classroom teachers are skilled in providing. Classroom music can also develop creative activities such as improvisation and composition – both of which benefit from the interaction of members of a larger group. Yet instrumental lessons can develop some aspects of pupils' musicianship – detailed technical and performance skills, for example – in ways that the classroom environment does not. Thus the two types of music education complement each other.

> **As their playing develops, children need a wider knowledge of many kinds of music, which classroom teachers are skilled in providing.**

The relationship between classroom music and instrumental lessons

For children who learn their instrument at school, classroom music and instrumental lessons often fit well together. Instrumental teachers, while not usually part of the permanent school staff, are aware of the school curriculum and what is happening in the classroom, and classroom music staff are usually keen to develop links with the school's instrumental teaching. Indeed, various initiatives by government and music-education bodies in the UK have focused on the interchange of ideas between classroom music teachers and their instrumental colleagues. The quality of instrumental teaching in school is monitored, assessed and inspected by school staff and government bodies in much the same way as other subjects are. Children who have instrumental lessons in a group (see Chapter 6) will find that their instrumental lessons more closely resemble what happens in classroom music.

Other instrumental pupils, particularly those who learn privately, may find the relationship between classroom music and instrumental lessons less clear. There are a number of reasons for this. Firstly, instrumental teachers have the specific goal of providing pupils with particular technical and musical skills; classroom music has other aims and covers different topics. Secondly, school music follows a generally recognized and assessed curriculum, which private music teachers are not obliged to do. (Many private teachers are familiar with music education in school and some use instrumental schemes that reflect this, but others work in different ways and have different priorities.) Thirdly, during one-to-one instrumental lessons a pupil has the teacher's undivided attention, while in class each individual is part of a large group of children with a broad range of skills, interests and cultural backgrounds.

▼▼▼ WEBWORDS "national curriculum" + music + mycountry

Other practical factors, such as the class size, the pupils' level of interest and their behaviour, will also affect the success or otherwise of a classroom music lesson. As a result, children learning an instrument may have to deal with two separate ways of learning music. This will probably not cause problems for your child, who may just compartmentalize the two, particularly if he or she is very young. However, difficulties can arise if your child is taught music one way in the classroom, and another way in instrumental lessons.

In order to learn effectively, children need to feel able to trust their teachers, and this is difficult if two teachers seem to be saying conflicting things. Each teacher might in fact be right, but children might not be able to reconcile apparently different points of view. Terminology offers an obvious example. There are two different systems of describing note lengths: one, based on note divisions, uses terms like half note, quarter note and so on; in the other, notes of different lengths have individual names: minim, crotchet and so on. Even though each system is equally valid, a child introduced to both systems by different teachers is liable to be confused.

Bringing it all together

Ideally, all aspects of a child's musical life – and all ways of learning – should support and develop each other. Any possible conflict can be avoided if your child's classroom music teachers are aware of your child's music activities elsewhere. Equally, instrumental teachers should know what is going on in class music lessons and other school music activities. Instrumental teachers can support these in a number of ways – helping a pupil with a piece he or she is playing with the school band or orchestra, for example.

Indeed, an instrumental teacher should know as much as possible about each pupil's experience of music in school. Your child can tell the instrumental teacher what sort of music activities take place in lessons, for example, and the teacher may make some interesting connections: if the class is listening to a particular piece, the teacher may find a version of it for the pupil to play; if a pupil writes music in classroom lessons, the instrumental teacher might play, or help the pupil to play, the composition; if a pupil is learning to improvise in school music, this might be further developed in the instrumental lesson. These kinds of activities will help to bridge the gap and bring the two sets of music lessons closer together.

An instrumental teacher should know as much as possible about each pupil's experience of music in school.

Some practical issues

Pupils who learn their instrument at school can run into difficulties if instrumental lessons are held during normal curriculum time. Staff normally support pupils leaving class for music lessons, but timetabling conflicts can be worrying for your child, and there may also be anxiety about missing a school lesson. For this reason, as a child's schoolwork burden increases, teachers usually take care that instrumental lessons do not clash with the teaching of core subjects.

School music-making will make demands on your child's time (and possibly on yours if you need to make extra journeys to or from school), so watch out for signs that your child is finding this stressful. But if your child wants to take part, do everything you can to make it possible: one of the most important reasons for learning an instrument is to be able to experience making music with others.

Bear in mind that children can find it hard to prioritize if their lives fill up with many extra activities – such as band or orchestra rehearsals on top of instrumental practice. Teachers are usually understanding during times when children are particularly busy (for instance in the days before a concert), but parents should manage these situations carefully.

Key points

- School can provide children with a wide range of music activities.
- In the UK, all children up to the age of 14 learn music in class – after that it is usually available as an optional examination subject.
- Classroom music and instrumental lessons usually fit together well, but look out for possible differences of approach that might confuse your child.
- Try to forge links between your child's music experiences inside and outside school, and encourage your child to do so too.

Chapter 11

MUSIC BEYOND THE LESSON

It is vital that young people enjoy their music lessons. If they do, it is a sign that things are going well. The true purpose of lessons, however, is to provide pupils with the means to get lifelong pleasure from music and making music with others. As children begin to make music outside the lesson, they start to reap the benefits of everything they are learning. Enjoyable, social music-making will motivate the pupil to continue, and any activity of this sort will be enormously beneficial to your child's musical development.

This chapter looks at:

- types of music-making activity available to young people
- who provides these activities
- getting access to these activities
- deciding whether an activity is right for your child
- activities that you and your child can organize

Types of music-making activity available to young people

The most common types of musical activity available to children are those devoted to 'practical' music-making – playing or singing with others. There are many choices, and the following should help you to decide which best suits your child.

Band any group of people who play together. A *brass band* is made up almost exclusively of brass instruments, though it usually includes some percussion players too. Brass bands play a wide range of music. Much of it is specially written for them in a variety of styles, but they also play arrangements of classical and popular pieces. A *military band* will include some woodwind instruments as well as brass and percussion; it may be run by a cadet force or similar organization and may involve marching while playing. Many military bands play a lot of ceremonial music – marches and fanfares for special occasions, for example – but play arrangements of the classics, show tunes and lighter music as well. A *concert band* or *wind band* combines woodwind, brass and percussion. Its range of music encompasses original pieces, classical arrangements, show tunes and pop music. A *big band*, which is mainly brass instruments (trumpets and trombones) with some woodwind (notably saxophones) and a rhythm section (piano, guitar, bass and drums), mostly plays jazz, dance-band and show music. A *jazz band* may range from just a few instruments (for example saxophone, trumpet, clarinet and rhythm section) to something rather larger but still with the same kinds of instruments. Of course, the word 'band' is also used in pop and rock music – sometimes inter-changeably with 'group' – to mean any smaller collection of singers and players.

Chamber music see *Ensemble*

Choir any group of people who get together to sing. Singing in a choir helps all musicians to understand music, whether they are primarily singers or not, because it encourages listening skills: each singer needs to hear how his or her part in the music fits within the complete sound. There are many kinds of choir – a *church choir* usually provides music for religious services; a *chorus* is usually a large group of singers who may perform in concerts, often accom-panied by an orchestra or other ensemble; a *chamber choir* is a smaller group of singers. The word 'choir' is more rarely used to describe a group of people all playing the same instrument (*clarinet choir* or *flute choir*, for example).

72

Ensemble any small- to medium-sized group of players or singers. An ensemble can be made up of any combination of instruments and voices. In classical chamber music in particular there are some standard groups – such as the *string quartet* (two violins, viola, cello), the *wind quintet* (flute, oboe, clarinet, bassoon, horn) and the *piano trio* (piano, violin, cello). But there is a vast quantity of interesting music available for virtually any instrumental combination in a wide variety of styles. Music festivals (see Chapter 15) often have classes for ensembles: this usually means anything from duets (two people) to octets (eight people).

Group a rather looser term for any combination of musicians – which may include voices, instruments or both. As well as pop, jazz and contemporary music groups, you may encounter *opera groups* (professional or amateur organizations that perform operas, musicals and shows). Some *drama groups*, while their emphasis is on theatre, perform shows and musicals. Musicians can also be required to supply incidental music for theatre productions. In school, many younger pupils have the opportunity to join a *recorder group* or a *percussion group* – these often teach the basics of music while giving children a first experience of music-making with others.

Orchestra a larger group of instrumentalists, usually (but not always) playing classical music. A *symphony orchestra* may be 100 or more players and will include woodwind, brass, percussion and string instruments; a *chamber orchestra* is a smaller version, usually with around 30 people; a *string orchestra* is made up only of string instruments – violins, violas, cellos and double basses.

The larger of the groups described above will be led by a conductor or director – a musician who supervises rehearsals and decides which music will be played and how it should be performed. The method and approach of conductors and directors varies: some feel that an easy-going, relaxed manner gets the best results, while others – particularly those who run very large groups – may feel it necessary to be stricter in order to keep everyone's attention. In all cases conductors or directors will demand respect and good behaviour from their players. Conductors are not common for small chamber-music, jazz and pop groups, the members of which usually agree on their own approach. However, in an educational context (such as at school or music college) even these small groups are likely to be supervised and coached by an expert player.

Other classes, workshops and groups Many organizations provide classes which help children to develop a great range of musical skills and disciplines. These include classes on history and theory; styles of music from around the world (practical sessions may be part of this); composition and improvisation; music technology; and rather more specialized aspects of music education such as Dalcroze or solfège. Such classes put instrumental learning in context and may inspire broader musical interests. They can also deliver aspects of your child's music education that may be missing from school or instrumental lessons. For example, to take an instrumental exam at the higher grades, pupils may first need a theory qualification. While many instrumental teachers teach theory, others prefer to concentrate on the practical aspects of their pupils' training. Sending your child to a dedicated theory class can therefore be very valuable.

73

> **Other classes can deliver aspects of your child's music education that may be missing from school or instrumental lessons.**

Who provides these activities?
Many different types of organization provide extra-curricular music activities for your child. These include:

- school
- local education authority music centres
- private music schools
- music colleges
- community organizations
- holiday courses

School In addition to classroom music lessons (see Chapter 10), many schools provide lunchtime and after-school music sessions for their pupils. The types of activities available are likely to depend on the size of the school, the age of the pupils and the availability of staff members to run the sessions. Many primary schools will run a recorder group and a choir, while older children may be able to take part in orchestras and bands; choirs; pop, rock and dance groups; and productions of shows and plays. Nearly all schools provide some of these, but while some schools are justifiably proud of their music and organize many activities for pupils, others have different priorities and music may be less important.

Local education authority music centres Many local education authority music services in the UK provide at least one music centre where children of all ages can go to make music – usually on a Saturday but sometimes on weekday evenings as well. There is usually a wide range of activities available for all abilities: most music services run orchestras, choirs, string groups, wind bands, ensembles, rock bands, jazz bands and theory classes. These are often carefully programmed and coordinated so that pupils can take part in a variety of groups and classes. Many centres also organize music schemes and courses in the school holidays, put on concerts and other performances, offer lessons in music technology and recording (see Chapter 12), and run other one-off events.

▼▼▼ WEBWORDS mycounty OR myborough + "music service"

Music centres have many advantages: teaching is undertaken by professionals approved by the local authority; participants will meet other enthusiastic children (often from outside their immediate social circle); and groups and activities are usually graded and organized to allow your child to move smoothly from one level to the next.

Participants will meet other enthusiastic children, often from outside their immediate social circle.

Private music schools There are many private music schools all over the world that provide a combination of instrumental tuition, group work, bands, orchestras and singing, as well as lessons in theory and other subjects. Many of these are small, self-contained organizations run by a group of teachers (or by charities or trusts). Others are part of a larger chain of music schools, some of which are managed by musical instrument manufacturers or large music retail outlets. Private schools may concentrate on a particular style or aspect of music: some specialize in pop, rock and dance music; others train students in all aspects of music technology and recording techniques.

▼▼▼ WEBWORDS music + school OR college + mytown

Private schools have certain advantages. Because they often have their own premises, they can be open for longer periods (many local authority centres operate on school premises which can only be used when the school is empty). They may therefore be more flexible when it comes to scheduling lessons and groups, and may be able to deliver a custom-made programme of study. While most teachers who work at private music schools will be both reputable and highly able, the quality of teaching may vary because these organizations are less subject to monitoring by a central educational body.

Music colleges Music colleges (or conservatoires) are higher education institutions where students can go to study music after leaving school (see Chapter 19). Many of them have junior (or preparatory) departments for younger pupils. These usually operate on Saturdays and provide a wide range of musical activities. The teachers will be part of the conservatoire staff so the standard of teaching is likely to be very high; your child will also be coached and encouraged to participate in a great deal of music-making. Any child accepted at a junior department is usually expected to undertake all music training there, including individual instrumental lessons. Entry is very competitive and fees may be substantial (although financial assistance is sometimes available), so application to one of these organizations is quite a big step. (There is more about this in Chapter 18.)

Community organizations All kinds of independent community groups run music activities or have need of musicians. Churches and other religious organizations have choirs and music groups. These range from small, highly trained choirs which provide the music for services to larger groups which meet and rehearse for pleasure. (Young singers who join formal church choirs may also receive training in aspects of music besides singing – such as theory and history.) There are also many amateur orchestras, bands and choirs which are established by groups of individuals solely for the enjoyment of music-making. And amateur operatic or dramatic groups often need singers or players to provide music for their productions.

WEBWORDS **mytown + church + choir OR mytown + community + music** ▼▼▼

Holiday courses There are several types of holiday course for instrumentalists and singers. Local education authorities often run them for many different instruments and musical styles, and many private organizations offer courses on a variety of music topics. Many are residential, but others, such as those provided by local music centres, require daily non-residential attendance over a period of a week or so. Particularly talented older children may be interested in one of the many high-powered international courses.

For most courses, your child will need to be at a particular level, and the course information should explain what this is (your child's teacher can advise here). Residential courses are only appropriate if your child is comfortable staying away from home, though every effort is made to make children feel welcome, entertained and secure.

WEBWORDS **holiday + music + course (+ myinstrument)** ▼▼▼

Getting access to these activities

Your child's instrumental teacher is the first person you should ask about suitable music-making activities. He or she will be familiar with your child's tastes and abilities and, as part of the music education community, will probably know what is on offer locally. If your child learns at school, his or her instrumental teacher is likely to be involved in the music centre and other local education authority activities, and is therefore a very good source of information. If you yourself find an activity, it is still wise to consult the teacher about its suitability. Some teaching methods and types of activity may be incompatible with the way in which your child is being taught.

Libraries or the offices of local (or national) government departments of leisure, arts or culture are good sources of information about community activities. Local newspapers or magazines may be useful too. The Internet can help, particularly if you are researching national and international courses. And don't forget word of mouth – ask other pupils (and parents) what they enjoy, and what they recommend.

Whether or not they are run by educational establishments, most of these activities (with the exception of holiday courses) will operate roughly in line with the school year. Some accept enrolment all year round, others at the start of each term, others only at the beginning of the academic year. Some may have a formal enrolment policy (particularly those run by educational organizations); for a few others, it may be sufficient to turn up, speak to the person in charge, and begin playing or singing – but this arrangement is rare.

Deciding whether an activity is right for your child

Many issues will affect how you and your child choose a suitable activity. Here are the main points to bear in mind:

- your child's age, ability and standard
- your child's desire to take part
- making the time
- cost
- practicalities

Your child's age, ability and standard Some groups and activities are open to all children, regardless of their age or standard – many school orchestras or choirs, for example, will admit any pupils who show an interest. Music centres and private music schools are also likely to be open to all, and will have a range of activities suitable for particular ages and standards. The supervisors and teachers will recommend the best groups or classes as each individual enrols, and may then move young musicians into other groups as their skills develop.

Other organizations may be more selective. A community choir or orchestra (and even some school orchestras) may have a minimum age or particular entry standard. Some orchestras and bands specify that membership is only open to players who have passed a particular grade exam (see Chapter 14); this is a straightforward way of ensuring a minimum level of ability. As children move up to more senior groups – such as the area bands and orchestras made up of the more advanced players from schools and music centres – competition for places increases. The standard is usually maintained by means of audition, whereby those in charge of the ensemble listen to and evaluate each candidate.

In most cases the audition system will be made clear to you during your initial enquiries. Children tend to understand the need for such selection processes and will usually be happy to comply. Remember, though, that competition can be very high for places in advanced orchestras, bands and ensembles, and you may well need to handle carefully the disappointment that your child will feel if he or she doesn't succeed.

At the junior department of a music college, the standard will be high and entry always by audition. Holiday courses also may request that students have reached a particular standard, and may be restricted to children above a certain age – particularly if the course is residential.

Although some classes and courses cater for absolute beginners, many require a very basic knowledge of a subject before the student can enrol. This is particularly true of certain technology classes. If your child wants to learn to use a particular piece of music software, for instance, a level of familiarity either with the program or with music theory is likely to be necessary.

Your child's desire to take part Some children will have a strong desire to join an orchestra, band or choir. Others may not yet be aware of the opportunities. Often the suggestion will come from your child's teacher – or from you yourself, if you have a musical background. Many children embrace these opportunities with great enthusiasm, but a few may be uneasy about unfamiliar activities, people or surroundings. Reassure your child by describing what will happen (or ask the teacher to do so), and by answering any questions. It is usually possible to visit a music centre or school, or to watch a choir or orchestra rehearse before deciding to join. Anything that makes the activity more accessible and more familiar will help build your child's confidence (attending with a friend should alleviate any worries about 'fitting in'). Older children may have insecurities about whether they will make friends, find the music too hard to play, and so on. Once more, careful explanation and gentle encouragement will help.

Anything that makes the activity more accessible and more familiar will help build your child's confidence.

Most children join in these activities without the slightest worry and will greatly enjoy the experience. Children are kept constantly occupied and there may be few breaks. This can be exciting, but it may be bewildering for some. Occasionally activities may be more relaxed, and while some children thrive when left to organize themselves, others become bored and lose direction. Find out as much as possible beforehand so that you and your child can make an informed choice about whether an activity is appropriate. Again, there is no substitute for talking to children who are already involved, or their parents.

Making the time Music-making with others takes up time and often demands a serious level of commitment. Over a period of weeks or months members become familiar with the music, and with the methods, interpretation and procedures employed by the group's director. The success of an orchestra, choir or group very much depends on the regular attendance of its members. An individual's absence holds the group back, because the conductor will need to revisit material already dealt with. Many bands and orchestras have rules about attendance, and it is important to be aware of these and respect them. The commitment may not just have implications for your child – if he or she needs transport to or from a rehearsal, a parent or other adult will have to be available on a regular basis. You may spend much of your time running an informal taxi service!

Music-making with others takes up time and often demands a serious level of commitment.

Orchestra or band members are usually expected to practise their music between rehearsals. Young people tend to enjoy playing with others but can find learning their individual part rather less exciting; this is where instrumental teachers can help out. Your child will find participation all the more satisfying if he or she is not struggling to play the notes.

Upon joining a band or orchestra, your child should receive a rehearsal schedule together with the dates of any concerts, performances or open days. Try to give as much support and encouragement as possible – particularly by attending concerts or other performances.

Cost The cost of these activities varies enormously. Most out-of-hours school activities will be free, though a small sum may be charged if teaching or coaching has to be provided by external teachers. A local education authority music centre is likely to make a small charge each term, though free places may be available under certain circumstances. Private music schools will charge higher fees, though subsidized places may be available. Fees for the junior department of a music college tend to be quite high because they include high-calibre instrumental tuition, and a full programme of activity. Again, subsidies, grants and scholarships are sometimes available. Holiday courses vary widely in cost, depending on their duration, whether they are residential or not and so on. Many community activities are free, although some charge a small fee which may go towards administration, venue rental costs, the conductor's fee or hire of music. There might be other necessary expenditure, ranging from travel costs to purchase of a band uniform, for example.

Practicalities Consider also the practical aspects of these activities. For example, young children need to know that they will arrive on time with all the equipment they require. (As well as an instrument and music, your child may have to bring food, pencils, a notebook, special shoes if dance is involved, computer storage media etc.) In some instances it might be easier for you to deliver your child to rehearsal and wait to collect him or her at the end. If so, find out whether the organization is happy for you to remain on the premises (a few may encourage parent volunteers to help). Also make sure that your child is comfortable with your presence. Many children, as they grow in confidence, prefer more independence.

79

> **Young children need to know that they will arrive on time with all the equipment they require.**

Activities that you and your child can organize

Don't forget the music activities that young people can devise for themselves – with your help if necessary. These include:

- making music with friends
- forming a band or group
- organizing a concert
- going to professional concerts and gigs

Making music with friends This can range from very informal activities – singing and practising dance steps to music or a morning spent playing piano duets, for example – to regular music-making at someone's home.

Forming a band or group Older children in particular may well want to form their own band or group with their friends. Whether your child wishes to set up a string quartet in the kitchen, organize a rock band in the loft or DJ informal club nights in the garage, try to find the time and space (and start sweet-talking the neighbours); this is music-making in action. Teenagers will want to do this unsupervised and with little attention from anyone else, but they are, all the time, developing musical, organizational and creative skills.

Organizing a concert Once a young player has learned and then performed a piece for an exam or concert it is usually abandoned. This is a shame. Children need to build up a stock of pieces that they can enjoy playing again and again, so encourage your child to put on occasional concerts with a few friends. These can be very informal, in front of a small audience of family and friends, and don't need to last long. The performers might like to design and produce a programme on a computer, perhaps with some information about the music (this encourages them to learn something about the pieces they are playing). You could treat everyone to drinks and snacks afterwards to increase the sense of occasion.

Older children may want to perform more independently. Playing in public really helps young musicians to grow in confidence. (See Chapter 13 for more about this.) If your child and friends want to set up a more formal concert, you and the other parents could hire a local hall or room in a community centre; perhaps your child's school would allow use of its hall. This can be a good way of trying exam or audition pieces, or music that the performers have composed themselves; and two or three performers together will provide a very good concert. Other places may be glad to host performances by young musicians, both formal and otherwise – leisure centres, residential and care homes for the elderly, hospitals, libraries and shopping centres.

Planning and organizing a concert teaches a broad range of musical and non-musical skills. Making sure that everyone is in the right place at the right time with all the necessary instruments and equipment is itself a challenge. Consideration also has to be given to the music's suitability for the particular audience; the running order of the musical items; attracting an audience; creating posters, tickets (if appropriate), and a programme booklet including information about the music and the performers; and perhaps even managing the finances.

Planning and organizing a concert teaches a broad range of musical and non-musical skills.

Going to professional concerts and gigs The importance of taking your children to live music events where they can experience the exciting atmosphere and be in the company of professional musicians cannot be overestimated. Many orchestras and venues organize pre-concert talks, open rehearsals and demonstrations (some specifically for children) during which the audience has the opportunity to meet the musicians and learn about the music to be played in the concert. Professional musicians are usually delighted to meet and encourage young players. Some may meet members of the audience and sign autographs after concerts, but this depends on the venue and the performer's schedule. If your child is keen to meet a particular performer check in advance whether this will be possible. Older children may prefer to go to concerts and gigs unaccompanied or with a group of friends.

Key points
- Any music-making with others will be of real benefit to your child's musical development.
- There are many types of activity run by many types of organization.
- To get access to these activities, start by asking your child's music teacher – school, libraries and the Internet can also be good sources of information.
- Consider your child's age, ability and desire to take part, as well as the cost and other practicalities.
- Many activities can be time-consuming but they are likely to be very rewarding too.
- There are plenty of music-making activities that you and your child can organize yourselves.

Chapter 12

MUSIC AND TECHNOLOGY

Technology is all around us. It is a fundamental part of children's lives – at home, at school and on the move. Many children take for granted access to a computer, a mobile phone, and something to record and play back music for personal use. They are likely to use the Internet as a standard resource for communication, entertainment and education. They may also have video equipment, electronic musical instruments, and the means to make music on a computer. Technology can enhance and expand an individual's experience of music in a huge variety of ways. The technological world moves fast, and products change rapidly. While this chapter does briefly discuss some types of technology, it is not a list of products or an introduction to their use: instead it concentrates on ways in which young musicians can integrate all types of electronic equipment into a general music education.

Children's knowledge and experience of technology is likely to be beyond that of their parents and most teachers. They may also be naturally able to understand new software and devices. Parents should try not to let their preconceptions of what technology can and can't do (and should and shouldn't do) limit their children's creative experiences – a child's curiosity about technology should be allowed to work as a stimulus to making music and learning about it.

Technology can enhance and expand an individual's experience of music in a huge variety of ways.

Using technology in music

Many people feel that computers and other electronic equipment are good education aids simply because the machines themselves stimulate interest. It is often argued that this is 'learning in disguise' – while children are enjoying using the computer, they are absorbing information about the subject in question as well. This may be true, but for an activity to have a real educational benefit children do have to know what is happening when they use equipment and understand how to reproduce its functions and effects in other contexts.

This necessarily involves a lot of exploration and experimentation – much of which you may not understand unless you know the technology yourself. Nevertheless, it can help if you understand the five basic ways in which technology can help young musicians:

- encouraging and improving practice
- enhancing performances
- enabling creative music-making
- providing practical help
- providing additional learning resources

Encouraging and improving practice Children may like to keep a practice record on the computer, noting the time, date and length of each session; their overall intentions for each practice; which pieces, exercises and scales were practised; and perhaps any problems they encountered (possibly to take back to the teacher for the next lesson). Younger children will enjoy 'filling in the boxes' on their chart – and this may also motivate older children to think carefully about what exactly they are achieving, to vary their practice routines and to make sure that they are connecting all aspects of their playing. Over a period of time this sort of document can form a record of your child's development, revealing strengths and weaknesses. Your child's teacher may also be prepared to take part, using a computerized 'practice record' instead of a notebook.

Technology can aid and improve practice in more directly musical ways. For example, some children find practising scales and arpeggios a chore, while others find it hard to keep the strict pulse that is necessary for accurate playing. Traditionally the advice has been to use a metronome – a mechanical or electronic device which clicks the beat to help the player stay in time. Technology now offers other more interesting methods. The automatic rhythm section on even the simplest electronic keyboard will provide a wide range of percussion backings to use in this way; a child simply sets the backing running and then plays over the top, adjusting the speed to suit his or her abilities. This promotes rhythmic accuracy and also develops awareness of other lines of music – and many children will enjoy monitoring the increasing fluency and speed of their scales. Similarly, you can buy publications – usually specific to a particular instrument – which contain the music for scales and a recording of backing tracks. And children who have access to sequencing or notation products on a computer (see below) could create their own backings for this activity. Another extremely effective practice aid, in terms of helping children's awareness of their strengths and weaknesses, is recording (see 'Enhancing performances' below).

Practising pieces can also be made more fun by playing along with the accompaniment. The accompaniments to many pieces are now published on CD or may be available to download, so your child need not rely on a live

83

pianist. In addition to the accompaniment there will usually be a recording of the complete piece for you to hear how the whole performance should sound. There may also be a slower version so that your child can practise playing along at a reduced speed until he or she has gained confidence. Ask your child's teacher about this sort of product. If a recording of the accompaniment is not commercially available you might be able to organize your own – perhaps your child's teacher or another musician would be prepared to make a CD or MP3 recording.

Accompaniments are available in other formats too. You may be able to acquire MIDI files of a particular piece; these are available in music stores and on the Internet, or your child's teacher may be able to create them. They can be played back on a computer and, with the appropriate (and inexpensive) software, can be speeded up, slowed down, rearranged for different instruments, put into different keys and so on. Other computer software can accompany the live instrument in an 'intelligent' way, speeding up and slowing down to match the natural ebb and flow of the performance. Systems like this can be extremely sophisticated, offering advice to pupils, pointing out mistakes, and providing the option of storing and sharing a recorded file of the performance.

▼▼▼ WEBWORDS "MIDI accompaniments" (+ myinstrument
OR composer's surname OR title of piece)

It is important to note that while recorded accompaniments are an excellent practice aid, your child must also practise unaccompanied, working carefully at smaller details and paying the fullest attention to the sound he or she is making.

Enhancing performances You or your child can make sound or video recordings using many different methods, using anything from very simple devices (such as a mobile phone) to the most sophisticated equipment. This has many advantages. Firstly, any use of technology to capture a performance teaches children about the equipment – positioning the camera, microphone or instrument; setting recording levels to get the best sound; and organizing signals to start and stop the recording. Secondly, it will encourage the performer to think about presentation – waiting until the machine is running to start playing; considering what to do before and after the music is performed; and thinking about how the music will sound (and look) to an audience. Thirdly, pupils benefit from hearing or watching themselves play. Because playing music requires the coordination of many technical matters (posture, sound production, precise finger work, and so on) and several musical and theoretical matters (such as reading the notation, playing expressively and conveying the music's character), young people sometimes lose sight of themselves as performers.

Young people sometimes lose sight of themselves as performers – an audio or video recording can help.

Making recordings can be very revealing and can help children to evaluate their performances, appreciating the good aspects and noticing areas that could be improved. A teacher may make observations about a pupil's playing that the child is unable to observe or understand – a recording makes these points clear to the child both quickly and effectively. Encourage your child to think about the performance and discuss the good points together with those that may require attention. In this way, making a regular audio or video recording will help your child's progress. This is particularly useful when, for example, an exam or concert performance is imminent. Of course recordings can easily be sent by email to friends, family and teachers, and used by children in their own creative efforts – as part of their own music productions and compositions, for example.

Enabling creative music-making Technology has made a great range of creative music-making activities available to young musicians. Making use of much of the technology need not cost a lot of money: a basic mobile phone will allow the user to create his or her own ringtone; the simplest electronic keyboard will provide a variety of drumbeats, instrumental sounds and recording facilities; and a basic computer set-up may include elementary recording and sequencing software (if not, such programs are often available free on the Internet). Equipment like this enables children to invent music, play it back, refine it, store it, and share it with others. These activities promote self-expression, aid learning about the mechanics of how music is made, and encourage children to interact with music in ways other than simply playing it.

85

WEBWORDS recording OR sequencing + ▼▼▼
software + download (+ DAW + music)

There are many types of software that can be used to make music on a computer. Some are traditional notation-based systems in which the user inputs notes onto the screen, using either a mouse and a computer keyboard, or a music keyboard, or all three. The music can then be played back via the computer's audio system and can be saved, altered, printed, distributed at will, and even published on the Internet. Other software is more akin to a computer-based recording studio, enabling the user to record, mix and balance using sound generated by either the computer or external instruments, or both. More specialized software – often used for dance music – allows users to record or sample sounds and manipulate them into complex pieces. This sort of software – and any accompanying hardware – need not be expensive: even free programs can be extremely powerful and may well meet your child's needs.

Even free software can be extremely powerful and may well meet your child's needs.

However, all of this can be complicated – possibly more so for the adult than the child – and with so much choice it can be hard to know where to begin.

Find out what your child wants to do with the software and whether he or she has used it before (at school or at a friend's house, for example). Take advice if possible from experienced users, a music store or a teacher; review sites and forums on the Internet are also good sources of help. For younger users, a child-friendly product may be available which will be easy to master and quick to produce results. Otherwise, not many of the standard products are too complicated for a motivated teenager. It may be sensible to arrange for a series of lessons to help your child learn the software – many music schools (see Chapter 11) run appropriate courses. Alternatively, you or your child should once again be able to find advice and guidance on the Internet.

▼▼▼ WEBWORDS music + notation OR sequencing
OR recording + software + reviews

Providing practical help A computer can be of enormous practical help for a musician. You can use the Internet to find out about music groups, orchestras or bands in your area. It also offers many outlets for sheet music and software. Much of it is free, some of it can be ordered online for delivery by post, and some can be downloaded for a fee. Online you will also find files for download – in MIDI or other audio formats – that your child can use as an accompaniment. These files may have to be purchased.

▼▼▼ WEBWORDS "sheet music" + download (+ free)

Notation software can be used by your child to write out music for other musicians to play, and to transpose music (put it into a different key so that it can be played by a different instrument or sung by a higher or lower voice). Although this technology can be quite complex, it is fun to learn and will enhance your child's experience of music. Again, your child's instrumental or school teacher may be able to advise you.

There are a few words of warning here. Firstly, bear in mind that there is a lot of illegally reproduced music on the Internet: if you download material (in whatever format) that is someone else's copyright without permission, you are committing an offence in much the same way as if you photocopy a piece of music. While some sites are legitimate, many are not. Secondly, you may want to supervise your child's Internet use (or at least be aware of its purpose), and give some basic lessons in Internet safety. Any music activity found on the Internet needs to be checked as carefully as you would any other form of online community.

Providing additional learning resources There are many CD-ROM and online resources that will help your child learn about music in a wider context. They cover a great variety of subjects. The most common are about the theory and history of music, but you can also find content and resources about musical instruments (including their history and technology), styles of music from all over the world, and the lives of individual composers and performers. Other resources deal with technical issues related to playing a particular instrument or concentrate on specific aspects of music education such as ear-training (the development of a good musical ear) or memory work. Many of these resources are attractively presented and can help stimulate a child's interest.

If you are contemplating buying one of these, check your choice with your child's teacher first. If the product you have in mind differs too much from the teacher's technical approach, terminology or style, you may create unnecessary confusion. Also make sure that the technical level and reading age are appropriate (most children's products are quite carefully labelled).

The Internet is also a magnificent source of music of all types. There are countless sites on which music is available for download, a great deal of it free of charge. This can allow children to hear, make, share and interact with all kinds of music, and to pursue styles that particularly interest them. Many professional musicians, bands, orchestras and ensembles have their own sites which engage users in a variety of ways, offering opportunities to explore pieces, play musical games or write and record new music. But caution is needed here, too: while many sites make music files freely and legally available, others are less reliable. Try to make sure that any material you download is copyright free or that you pay for it legitimately – it is usually an offence to share files without the owner's permission.

The Internet is a magnificent source of music of all types.

87

Other benefits of technology

Social networking sites offer musicians the means to share and exchange their views, knowledge and understanding, their tastes, and the music they make. Some musicians have launched highly successful careers through these means alone. These sites can also provide a way for young people to receive comments on and reviews of their own playing, compositions, improvisations or writing about music. This is generally valuable and can help young musicians to grow in confidence and ability. However, as with any other topic on any social networking site, there is always the potential for malicious abuse – and any child receiving unfavourable reactions from strangers may become seriously demoralized.

Besides helping to broaden the understanding of music theory and practice, technology brings with it a number of other educational benefits. For example, because a computer is such a powerful resource, it can encourage children to become more independent, helping them to identify problems and enabling them to find solutions. Research skills – such as understanding how to find and exchange information on the Internet – are likely to be stimulated when working on a particular musical topic. Organizational and communication skills can be improved too – even a seemingly mundane matter like using email or a social networking site to schedule and organize rehearsals helps children to cooperate and communicate with each other to achieve a common goal. In this way, technology can also help a child's civic and community skills.

Key points

- Technology can bring huge benefits to children learning music, in many different ways.
- Children are likely to be more comfortable with technology than their parents, so be prepared not to understand what's going on.
- Children's natural creative curiosity about technology can be used to stimulate music-making and learning about music.
- The Internet is unmatched as a source of music and information about music, but make sure that your child is using it safely.
- When downloading and distributing files from the Internet, make sure that they are legal (and free from viruses).

88

Chapter 13

PLAYING IN PUBLIC

Sooner or later, your child is likely to have the opportunity to perform in public. This might be in a concert at school or the music centre, or at an event organized by your child's teacher or by you yourself. There may be the chance to play in a community setting such as a hospital, a care home for the elderly or a shopping centre. You should do whatever you can to encourage your child to take part, since playing for others is a vital part of music-making – and performing is a skill which requires courage and practice.

Many teachers and schools try hard to make performing a normal activity for children by scheduling frequent concerts (some formal, some less so) for parents and other pupils. This works well for many children – they like being in front of an audience and it stimulates them to do their best – but others may find the idea more intimidating. This chapter looks at how you can help to make public performances enjoyable and rewarding for your child.

Playing for others is a vital part of music-making.

Preparing to perform

A good performance in a concert can be extremely motivating and rewarding. On the other hand, a child who feels a sense of underachievement – or worse, embarrassment – after a concert may be demoralized and demotivated for a long while. To get the most out of any public performance, therefore, a child must be properly prepared in order that stress, nerves and the potential for mistakes are minimized.

A little nervous excitement is normal and even desirable.

A little nervous excitement is normal and even desirable (it shows that your child is taking the event seriously), and indeed most children take public performance in their stride. If the prospect of performing frightens or distresses your child, however, be sympathetic and try gently to get to the root of the problem. It is usually unwise to force children to perform if they are genuinely against the idea.

The best way to keep anxiety to a minimum is to know as much as possible about the event beforehand. Practical information will normally be provided by the concert organizers, the child's teacher or the leader of the group or ensemble. But children often forget important details or remember them only at the last minute, so you may need to familiarize yourself with what is to happen as well. Try not to fuss – making too big a deal of the event may have a negative effect on your child – but find out as much information as you can. Below are a few things to think about before your child takes the stage:

- date, time and venue
- accompaniment
- equipment, accessories and supplies
- dress code
- preparation for going on stage
- what to do on stage

The best way to keep anxiety to a minimum is to know as much as possible about the event beforehand.

Date, time and venue Make sure that you know when and where the concert is; the transport or parking arrangements; what time your child has to be there (there may be a rehearsal beforehand); what time it will end; and, if you can't be in the audience, whether you need to arrange to collect your child at a particular time.

Accompaniment If your child is playing a solo and needs an accompanist, you or the teacher will have to find someone to accompany and, if possible, rehearse with your child. If your child is playing to a backing track (on a CD, for example), you need to know that the appropriate equipment is available and that someone will be operating it.

Equipment, accessories and supplies Check whether your child needs to take anything to the concert besides an instrument and music – are music stands provided, for instance? If your child is a pianist, try to ensure that the piano is at least playable: while you can't expect a top-of-the-range concert grand, your child deserves better than an out-of-tune instrument with dirty keys that stick. There should also be suitable chairs for children who have to sit down to play. A child playing a piece with a CD backing may be required to bring a CD player. Refreshments may or may not be provided, and you should discover if a packed lunch or tea is necessary.

Dress code If your child has a choice as to clothing (if school, band or other uniform isn't required), he or she may want to dress up to create a sense of occasion. With this in mind, you could buy or borrow some special concert clothes, and take advice from the teacher or organizers about what is suitable. Your child may want to make a big impression on the audience, and this is fine

– so long as it's appropriate for the occasion. Or your child may just want to fit in with the others, in which case you need to find out what everyone else will be wearing. Above all, stage clothes must be comfortable.

Preparation for going on stage Your child may need help in preparing his or her instrument for going on stage. Before an orchestral concert, adult helpers will normally be around to help tune and check instruments and provide last-minute reassurance. Otherwise, you may need to enquire who will help your child with this.

What to do on stage Once on stage, your child should know where to go, and whether to stand or sit; teachers or concert organizers will usually advise. There should always be time to adjust a music stand or microphone to the correct height; the audience will not mind waiting a short while, so your child should take his or her time and not feel the need to hurry. He or she should also know what to do with any accessories – such as a mute, or spare music (if playing more than one piece). And your child should have been taught how to respond to applause, and told when to leave the stage, and whether or not to return for an extra bow if the applause continues.

During and after the show
You should always try to be in the audience when your child is performing – this provides moral support and both reassures and motivates the child. Don't try, however, to attract his or her attention, as this can be distracting. Often it is enough for younger children to know that you are there, and it is best to sit, watch and listen reasonably discreetly, but join in the applause with enthusiasm. Be aware that your child might find it quite difficult to be the centre of attention, and feel uncomfortable about accepting public praise.

The audience might be a sea of video cameras, as many parents want to record their child's performance. This may be fine, but there are various things to consider. Firstly, it can be off-putting to your child (and any others on stage) to feel that they are being filmed; secondly, the organizers (or the venue itself) may have a policy preventing filming from taking place; and thirdly, you may enjoy the event more if you simply sit and absorb the experience. Live performances – particularly those given by your children – are very special occasions. If you are concentrating on filming, you may miss aspects of the show that are impossible to capture for the future.

After the performance, most younger children will instinctively make their way to their parents. Older children may prefer initially to spend time with the other performers and share the atmosphere of the event. When you do see your child, always begin by praising their performance, whatever the quality of the playing. Concerts are often a very intense experience for children, and afterwards they will need to hear your praise and encouragement and to feel

91

that you share their excitement. (While it's natural to feel that your child's performance was the most important, make sure that you praise the other children too.)

It is easy to be enthusiastic after a successful performance. But if there have been problems – and things do go wrong in concerts – your child may feel disappointed or even distressed. Do not dismiss these feelings but always counter them by saying how proud you are that he or she has taken part. It is extremely rare that a child's performance will embarrass you. Audiences are usually very sympathetic to young players, and neither you nor your child need to feel ashamed if things don't go well. Even if you do feel uncomfortable, take the greatest care not to transmit this to your child.

Your child may be excited and 'high' for some time after the concert. This is a result of the anticipation of the event, the concentration during it and also the relief that it is over. After an evening concert, it may be unrealistic to expect your child to go to bed immediately, so try to allow a little extra time for calming down. This might include giving your child a small treat to mark the event and show your appreciation of his or her efforts. If possible, talking about the event in detail should wait until the following day, by which time all concerned will have had time to process everything that happened. Your child's teacher, if present, will give you some feedback about your child's performance. And always ask your child's opinion of how it went; children are often excellent judges of their own work and that of others. If your child insists that you talk about any aspect that wasn't successful, proceed very carefully – you can easily damage self-confidence with a badly chosen remark. It is best to leave detailed criticism to the teacher if possible.

Always ask your child's opinion of how it went; children are often excellent judges of their own work and that of others.

Key points

- Playing in public is a vital part of music-making and a skill in its own right.
- Minimize the stress of performance by preparing your child thoroughly.
- A little nervousness is normal.
- Attend your child's performances if at all possible.
- Always praise your child's efforts, saving any constructive criticism for later or, better, leaving it to the teacher.

Chapter 14

MUSIC EXAMS

Society attaches great importance to exams and competitions, and the world of music is no exception. Whether they (or we) like it or not, pupils will be presented with plenty of opportunities to compete and be tested. Exams and competitions, when used responsibly, can motivate and energize your child's music-making and provide a real sense of achievement. This chapter looks at the uses and purpose of exams and how to help your child get the most out of them. Festivals and competitions are dealt with in Chapter 15.

The type of music exams discussed below are those intended for individual musicians. Yet much of the information here also relates in a more general way to a range of other exams and assessment schemes for groups. These include ensemble or choral exams, which are available from various organizations and assess a group's ability as a whole; and other schemes, such as ABRSM's Music Medals (available in the UK), which assess an individual's performance within a group context and the candidate's ability to perform and interact with other musicians.

How exams work

Instrumental music exams are normally run by independent organizations (known as 'boards') which are separate from those providing exams for the general school curriculum. These organizations are usually affiliated to establishments offering higher education in music (for example music colleges). The boards offer a range of graded exams for voice and most instruments, supply and train their own examiners, and undertake the administration for hundreds of thousands of exams a year worldwide. Some boards offer exams for different types of music (such as jazz and pop), as well as assessments for pupils taught in groups. Other smaller organizations – private music schools, for example, or specific training organizations such as church or community choirs – may have their own systems of tests, assessments or examinations.

WEBWORDS music + exam + board ▼▼▼

Most boards divide their exams into eight levels or grades. As the grade numbers increase, the exams become more challenging and a wider range of musical activities is tested. Some boards also offer preliminary tests which gently introduce young musicians to the exam system. For musicians who wish to pursue their studies beyond Grade 8, many boards and colleges offer diplomas (exams for advanced students; see Chapter 18 for more about this). The level of achievement indicated by a particular grade is broadly similar among the boards, but may not correspond exactly. In addition, some boards emphasize different aspects of musicianship and have slightly different approaches to exams. Many teachers therefore tend to develop a preference for one board's set of exams.

Exam boards publish their syllabuses and requirements well in advance of the actual exam period. This gives pupils plenty of time to prepare, though this time is not unlimited because syllabuses do change (some more often than others). Your child's teacher will probably inform you if he or she thinks your child is ready to take an exam. If you agree to this, you will be asked to purchase the pieces and other exam materials. Doing this commits you to nothing – if your child later decides not to take the exam, studying for it will still have been a valuable experience.

▼▼▼ WEBWORDS **myinstrument + exam + syllabus**

Nearer the exam period the teacher will formally enter the pupil for the exam, and you will have to pay an entry fee. The board will confirm the details of the date, time and venue. Exams usually take place at a local music centre, college or school – but church halls, hotels or private houses can also be used. During the exam, a qualified examiner (an experienced musician who has been appointed, trained and approved by the board in question) will listen to your child perform the prepared work, and will also examine other aspects of musicianship – such as aural tests, sight-reading and musical knowledge. (For more details, see 'What happens in a music exam?' below.) Boards vary in their delivery of the results – you may receive them at the end of the examination day, or via the teacher some weeks later.

Why take music exams?

Many teachers rely on the grade and diploma system of music exams to form the basis and structure of their teaching, so it is very likely that at some stage the opportunity to take an exam will be offered to your child. Music exams can provide:

- motivation
- an independent statement of achievement
- promotion of a balanced musical training
- useful feedback
- focus, consolidation and structure

Motivation Perhaps the most important aspect of a music exam is that it can be a powerful source of motivation. In preparing for and passing an exam, a pupil has to rise to a set of challenges, after which he or she can go on to study more demanding and exciting music. Passing the exam sets up a strong incentive to continue playing and learning.

> **Passing an exam sets up a strong incentive to continue playing and learning.**

An independent statement of achievement Exam boards both set and maintain consistent and measurable standards; they are externally accredited and provide an excellent independent assessment of a candidate's abilities. This means that teachers, parents and pupils are able to monitor progress by charting the musical and technical ability of a student against an existing set of standards. This has a number of advantages. Many orchestras, bands and ensembles limit membership to players of a certain grade or level – an orchestra insisting that all members have passed, say, Grade 5 before they join can thus ensure that all its members have a particular level of musical and technical expertise. Additionally, some education systems (including those in the UK) recognize instrumental music exams as qualifications which can be counted as part of a pupil's general educational record.

> **Instrumental music exams are often recognized as qualifications which count as part of a pupil's general educational record.**

Promotion of a balanced musical training Exam preparation involves study of many different aspects of music-making and musicianship. Since the candidate in an exam will need to display evidence of technique by playing scales, arpeggios and other technical material, these essential supporting disciplines will have to be developed alongside the practice and performance of pieces. Similarly, candidates will probably be asked to demonstrate aspects of general musicianship – by sight-reading or sight-singing, for example. If the pupil is to pass the exam these different aspects cannot be neglected, and this ensures that each examinee receives a broad and inclusive musical training.

95

Useful feedback For many pupils, an exam is an opportunity to perform in front of – and to have their playing assessed by – an independent and unbiased professional musician. Examiners are usually required by the examining board to offer some written feedback to the pupil as well as providing straightforward marks for each section of the exam. This feedback can be a valuable source of encouragement and advice (and sometimes it reinforces points that the teacher has already made).

> **The examiner's feedback can be a valuable source of encouragement and advice.**

Focus, consolidation and structure Exams can provide an excellent framework for learning. They require pieces, studies, technical work and a range of musicianship skills to be brought to a particular standard at a particular time – thus encouraging all-round musical development. And because they are set up to make increasing technical and musical demands as the candidate progresses through the grades, exams can also help to structure a longer-term course of study.

For a variety of reasons, some teachers feel that exams are inappropriate. Some rarely enter their pupils for exams, seeing them as an unnecessary burden or a distraction from other aspects of learning which they consider more important. Teachers may also judge that a particular pupil may respond negatively to the pressure and challenge of an exam. There are also occasions when a teacher might feel that entering an exam will clash with other important events in a pupil's life. You as a parent may or may not agree with what the teacher feels, and the best way forward is open and frank discussion.

Misusing exams

It is necessary to be aware of the problems that may result if the exam system is misused. Perhaps the most common of them occurs when pupils are fed a diet of exam material to the exclusion of anything else. Teachers who simply present pupils with one exam after another will cause a kind of musical malnutrition, which in turn may lead to a stunted musical growth. Ideally, learning music should involve the experience of a very wide range of music-making activities. Exams are an excellent way to motivate pupils and monitor their progress, but on their own they cannot provide the breadth of study necessary to produce completely rounded musicians. Most teachers agree that pupils who experience a broad range of musical activities are likely to do much better in exams than those whose sole focus and repertoire experience is exam-related.

Exams on their own cannot provide the breadth of study necessary to produce completely rounded musicians.

Entering a child for the wrong grade can be damaging – the grade has to be appropriate to the pupil's general musical ability. Of course the exam must be challenging, providing a real sense of achievement and personal reward, but candidates should only be entered where there is a strong probability of passing, and never simply to 'make them work harder' (this type of pressure is unlikely to produce a pupil's best performance). Exams are, first and foremost, for the benefit of the pupil, and putting a pupil through the exam process for the gratification of the parent or teacher is very unfair.

Certainly, children should never be entered for grade exams against their will. A lot of hard work is vital for success, and if children are not at least reasonably keen to take the exam, they will not be prepared to put in the necessary effort. Failure, for whatever reason, is discouraging and demoralizing for both teacher and pupil, and so the decision whether or not to enter a child must not be taken lightly.

What happens in a music exam?

Most exams follow a similar scheme and have similar requirements. While the material becomes more demanding as the grades increase, the basic components remain the same:

- performance of pieces
- scales and arpeggios
- sight-reading
- aural tests and musicianship
- other specific activities

Performance of pieces For each instrument and each grade, the syllabus will feature lists of pieces, often grouped together in different styles. The candidate (usually in consultation with the teacher) will eventually select one piece from each of three groups. A good teacher will allow his or her pupils to work on several of these pieces before making the final decision. At the exam, candidates will tell the examiner which pieces they have selected and will be asked to perform each one. The examiner will be listening for technical fluency, a stylish musical performance and the ability to convey the music's character.

For many instruments, and for singers, most pieces will require a piano accompaniment. This is an essential part of the exam and candidates will have to provide an accompanist: the examiner will not accompany the candidate. The accompaniment may be played by the pupil's teacher, or someone else previously chosen by the pupil and teacher (for whom you may have to pay). The success of a performance, especially in the higher grades, will be strongly influenced by the interaction between the two players, so it is important that, when preparing for the exam, your child gets as much experience as possible of playing with an accompanist.

> If an accompaniment is required, it is an essential part of the exam and you will have to provide an accompanist.

Scales and arpeggios For each exam the syllabus will list a number of scales and arpeggios (or other technical exercises) that the pupil must learn to play, usually from memory. It may also specify that the scales should be played in different styles. For example, a violin candidate may be asked to play scales 'separate bows' (one note to a bow) or 'slurred' (several notes to a bow). The candidate prepares all the necessary scales and arpeggios in advance of the exam, and needs to be ready to play any or all of them as requested by the examiner. The examiner will look for technical fluency – even and rhythmic playing, with good control of the sound.

Sight-reading In a sight-reading test the candidate is asked to play or sing a piece of music he or she has never seen before. A short period is allowed for the candidate to look at and try out the music before starting to play. The examiner assesses the pupil's ability to perform unfamiliar music convincingly. There are a number of ways in which pupils can improve their sight-reading skills – the teacher will advise – but there is no substitute for regular, methodical practice.

Aural tests and musicianship Aural tests examine candidates' ability to listen to music and understand what they hear; the content of the tests varies according to the board and the grade. The examiner may play short musical fragments on the piano and ask the candidate to repeat them by singing or playing, beat time or conduct, analyse simple harmony, sing or play an answering phrase, or answer a few short questions about musical theory or style. Most boards issue books of sample tests for practice purposes.

Other specific activities Some exams include a section in which candidates are asked questions about the pieces they have performed. And certain types of exam include tests specific to a particular instrument or style of playing. For instance, a candidate for a jazz exam will be expected to improvise; and a drum kit exam is likely to include a section during which the candidate plays along to unfamiliar music and chooses an appropriate drumming style.

Working towards exams

A pupil should never be plunged directly from one exam into another, and should only be entered for an exam after a period of broad development and preparation. Naturally the teacher will know how much work, and of what kind, will be involved in advance of the exam, and should explain it all carefully to the pupil. (Check with your child every so often that he or she is sure of what the exam will require; consult the teacher if there seems to be any doubt.)

You, as the parent, also need to be aware of the implications: after all, you will be looking after your child through all the hard work and stressful moments – and probably footing the bill too. The teacher will direct the pupil's work so that all the necessary areas are covered, but your child will need to practise hard and will need your support. In advance of the exam there are a number of practical things you can do to help:

• encourage performance
• help with practice
• inform your child
• keep the exam in perspective

Your child will need to practise hard and will need your support.

Encourage performance In order to succeed in exams, pupils need to feel confident about performing for others. Good teachers will always be trying to set up opportunities for performing exam and other pieces – the more of them the better. You can help by encouraging your child to play or sing for you, for family and for friends. If your child is happy to do this, take time to listen whenever possible. If your child asks for your opinion, always be positive and reassuring. Leave detailed comment to the teacher.

> **In order to succeed in exams, pupils need to feel confident about performing for others.**

Help with practice Encourage regular practice and ensure that all the areas of study are covered. You could help your child make a chart to show which scales have been studied and how often. Other practice aids are available too. You could find professional recordings of the pieces; some exam boards issue their own CDs of syllabus pieces, often supplying a piano accompaniment for solo instruments so that your child can practise playing along. (Pupils should avoid simply copying recorded performances, however. Instead they should use them to familiarize themselves with the music before developing a personal interpretation.)

WEBWORDS **myinstrument + exam + CD** ▼▼▼

Inform your child If your child has never taken an exam before, it is important that he or she has as clear an idea as possible about what will happen – from the practicalities of getting there to who will be in the room, how long it will last, what happens if something goes wrong, and so on. If you do not know these things yourself, ask the teacher. In addition, exam boards often publish freely available support materials to answer these questions and make the process easier to understand. Encourage your child to ask questions, too.

99

You can also help your child to experience the exam in advance by holding a mock exam at home, or more than one for a nervous candidate. Listen to all the pieces and scales, and give a sight-reading test – even if you have no idea whether your child is playing correctly or not. You can also buy recordings of sample aural tests for practice and to use in a mock exam. The more children know what to expect, the less nervous they will be.

Keep the exam in perspective It is right that you and your child should take the exam seriously, and everyone involved will be hoping for good results. But it is, after all, only an exam and should be seen as one small part of a larger music education. Try not to make your child feel that the exam is a crucial hurdle. For example, avoid offering incentives to do well because children often under-perform if they feel that too much is at stake. Praise your child's efforts as well as achievements. Think positively, and encourage your child to do so as well. Children who have a positive attitude are always likely to do better than those who are less well motivated.

An exam should be seen as only one small part of a larger music education. Praise your child's efforts as well as achievements.

The exam itself

The most important rule is to stay calm and relaxed. Encourage your child to get a good night's sleep before the day of the exam. On the day, try to remove as many practical causes of anxiety as possible. Make sure that you leave home with everything you need – all necessary music, the instrument (if appropriate) and any accessories (spare strings, rosin, reeds etc.). Check that the accompanist, if needed, knows when and where to meet you. If the exam is not taking place at school, be sure that you know where to go and that your child arrives at the exam centre with plenty of time to spare. The worry caused by the possibility of being late can be damaging. Try not to take anyone else along – it will keep things calmer if it is just you and your child.

When you arrive at the exam centre, a steward will probably register your child and direct you both to a waiting room until the examiner is ready. Do your best to appear calm yourself (even if you are not!), since anxiety is easily transferred from one person to another. Remaining as quiet and 'invisible' as possible will give your child time and space to concentrate and focus on the task ahead. Be sensitive and offer only encouragement and moral support, as confidence may need to be bolstered up. Have some relaxing strategies up your sleeve – taking deep breaths or sitting quietly with eyes closed can be a great help.

Your child will be given the opportunity to warm up and prepare for the exam in the waiting room (there may even be a piano or silent keyboard for pianists to do a little preparation) and tune the instrument if necessary. Doing the familiar warm-up routines will help to calm nerves. The steward will show the candidate (and accompanist) to the exam room, where there will be time to tune the instrument to the piano as required. Parents are expected to remain in the waiting room during the exam.

If the exam takes place in a large centre, there may be many people around. This may help as it can distract candidates from their nerves, but it has its disadvantages. For instance, you may hear rumours about the examiner, put about by candidates who have already taken their exams (or by their parents). Don't be tempted to join in – young children especially can become alarmed if they hear others saying that the examiner is strict or unfriendly. Such remarks are rarely accurate and never helpful. However, be sensitive and encouraging to other candidates and their parents – they are likely to be nervous too.

Practical hints for the day itself

Encourage your child to remember the following practical hints during the exam:

- Smile when entering the room, and greet the examiner; this immediately creates a positive atmosphere.
- If possible, take a bottle of water into the exam; this is especially useful for singers, and woodwind and brass players.
- Relax before you start to play, and take time to make sure that you are comfortable; if the music stand or stool is at the wrong height do not be afraid to adjust it or ask for help.
- If you are playing with an accompanist, make sure that you are both ready to begin.
- If you make a mistake, just try to keep going – but if you have to stop, relax and then continue; if you are near the beginning of the piece, you might ask the examiner for permission to start again.
- Between pieces, wait quietly until the examiner asks you to begin the next one.
- Don't worry if the examiner asks you to stop playing one piece and move onto the next; an examiner doesn't have to hear the entire piece to know that you play it well!
- If the examiner says something that you don't understand, ask him or her to explain.
- Make sure that you think about any questions you are asked before answering.

Marks and results

During the exam, the examiner will write a report about the candidate's playing and note down marks for each section. Candidates have to score a minimum number of marks to pass. Beyond that, they may be awarded higher levels of achievement – such as 'merit' or 'distinction' – if they score particularly well. Whatever the result, if children have been well prepared, and if the preparation has been rich in musical variety and experience, then the system has been put to effective use. Results are usually sent by post to the person who entered the pupil for the exam, anything from a day to a few weeks afterwards.

The result is a very useful guide to a child's level of attainment – it means that a certain general standard has been reached. While it's true that not everything about music performance can be measured, and not everyone hears in the same way, exam boards go to great lengths to train their examiners so that assessment is accurate, objective and consistent. This means that you can trust the result and what it says about your child's achievement on the day.

Do bear in mind that many factors may affect the outcome of the exam that have little to do with your child's musical ability. Each individual deals with the pressure of an exam in different ways, and those with self-confidence are likely to do better than those who suffer badly from nerves. In the run-up to the exam children may have found it difficult to fit everything into a busy life – or may be experiencing social or emotional problems at home, at school, or with relationships. And luck may play a part here: the examiner might happen to ask to hear the candidate's favourite scales; a disturbance outside the exam room might cause a break in concentration; or a reed or instrument might go wrong. However carefully an exam candidate is prepared, something unexpected may happen.

After the exam

For many children, preparing for the exam will have meant more intensive practice than usual, with the expenditure of much time and energy. Consequently, after the exam there will need to be a period of 'musical relaxation'. This is a good time to begin new pieces and to look at new technical areas; it may also be possible to learn duets or get involved in playing ensemble music. And a good teacher will help a pupil to consolidate any new musical ideas, techniques and concepts that were learned during preparation for the previous exam – so that, as and when the next one comes around, there will be a good base on which to build.

Key points

- Music exams can have a positive effect on a child's progress but they need to be used carefully.
- An exam tests many different aspects of a child's ability, not just playing pieces.
- Never enter a child for an exam against his or her will, and avoid going straight from one exam to the next without a break; a good teacher will know best what is suitable for your child, and when.
- Make sure that you and your child are sure of what is required for the exam – ask the teacher, and carefully read the syllabus and any supporting documents.
- Keep the exam in perspective: remember that it is only a small part of your child's general music education.
- On the day, remove as many stresses as possible and try to keep your child (and yourself) calm and relaxed.

Chapter 15

FESTIVALS AND COMPETITIONS

Music exams allow an individual's ability to be measured against internationally established standards. While this is a very useful means of monitoring progress and assessing achievement, it lacks an element of direct competition because examiners review candidates on their own merits, one at a time. Music festivals and competitions, however, assess the abilities of a group of entrants and award prizes to those who, in the opinion of the judge or judges, give the best performances. They also offer a valuable opportunity for developing musicians to perform in public, in front of an audience.

This chapter is about how festivals and competitions work, and how your child can get the best out of them.

What happens at festivals and competitions?

Music competitions and competitive festivals throughout the world range from modest local and regional events to high-profile international contests with considerable media coverage. Some take place once a year, others less frequently.

Local and regional events tend to encourage participation from a wide range of performers as a way of celebrating local talent, and may include other arts besides music (acting, poetry, dance, painting and sculpture, for example). For musicians there will be a range of 'classes', each dedicated to a particular voice or instrument, and then further divided into standards and ages. There may also be classes for ensembles, pop and jazz groups, or folk, traditional and ethnic music. Each festival will have its own approach to the range of classes on offer. More specialized national and international events (see 'High-profile competitions' below) usually have fewer classes, concentrate on fewer categories of performance (often just one instrument), and are likely to be restricted to entrants within a particular age range or of a particular standard. Many festivals also offer non-competitive classes, concerts and other events.

More than 300 festivals worldwide are affiliated to The British and International Federation of Festivals for Music, Dance and Speech, but there are many others besides. In addition, some schools, music centres and colleges, universities, local councils, arts groups, newspapers, broadcasting companies and other media run their own festivals. (These are often sponsored by businesses that provide prize money and other funds.)

Well in advance of any festival, the organizers will issue a programme or syllabus which lists the various events and classes and explains the terms and conditions of entry. It will also indicate the requirements for each class, such as age limit or standard, and say where and when each class is to take place. Some festivals (or classes) may prescribe set pieces; in others, candidates are free to choose their own piece or pieces (depending on the length of time allowed).

Entrants in each class will perform in front of an audience and are assessed by one or more expert adjudicators (judges) – usually experienced teachers and professional performers. Once all the performers have been heard, the judge(s) will give spoken comments about each, commonly in front of the audience, and name the winners. (Traditionally audience members have no influence over the result, though this is now not uncommon in pop competitions and other high-profile media events.) Prizes may be awarded to the outstanding performers: in smaller festivals, the prize may be a medal, a small gift or a trophy; in international competitions the winners often receive large sums of money, perhaps the chance to study with world-famous teachers, offers of recording contracts, and further opportunities for performance.

The practicalities

Finding out about festivals and competitions in your area is usually straightforward – try your library, local council or music centre. Here again the Internet can be useful, as a number of websites list competitions, both national and international. Your child's teacher should be aware of forthcoming festivals and competitions and may suggest entering. If it is not the teacher but you or your child that suggests entry, secure the teacher's agreement beforehand, since your child will need the teacher's help to prepare for the event.

▼▼▼ WEBWORDS music + festival (+ competitive OR competition) + mytown

The teacher will advise on which class or classes to enter and which pieces to perform. Some festivals are free; others charge a small entry fee to cover administration. Unlike in an exam, many festivals and competitions provide an accompanist for solo singers or instrumentalists, but you can bring your own accompanist if you prefer: this can be a parent, teacher or friend (restrictions are rare). Normally the entry form will ask whether you wish to use the official accompanist or not. Even if your child is using the official accompanist, it is vital that arrangements are made to practise with a pianist well before the performance so that your child is familiar with how the two instruments should sound together. On the day, as with an exam, it is important that you arrive in plenty of time and familiarize yourself with the arrangements. (See the list in Chapter 13 for suggestions about minimizing stress and anxiety before a performance.)

The benefits of festivals and competitions

Taking part in festivals and competitions can have many different, and sometimes unexpected, benefits for children (and for parents and teachers). These include:

- motivation
- experience of public performance
- meeting other musicians
- learning to compete
- confidence to persevere
- teamwork
- constructive and impartial feedback

Motivation As with music exams, preparing for a competition or festival focuses a pupil's mind on a particular event. Your child will spend time practising in order to rise to a particular set of challenges and, provided these are reasonable, this can be a great source of motivation. Festival performances may also act as a trial run for a grade or school exam. The competition itself is likely to be an important occasion for you, as a parent, too – an opportunity to hear your child perform and for you to show your support.

105

Experience of public performance Unlike exams, most festivals take place in front of an audience, often quite a large one. Musicians react to this in different ways, but performing for people is a vital part of learning to make music – children begin to think beyond lessons and practice, and to consider themselves as performers. Participating in festivals and competitions can be the main experience of public performance that some children have during their school years.

> Children begin to think beyond lessons and practice, and to consider themselves as performers.

Meeting other musicians Young musicians participating in a festival or competition will have an opportunity to meet other performers of varying ages; seeing and hearing what others can achieve often inspires children. They will also get the chance to hear music that is new to them, and to learn from, and perhaps meet, distinguished judges.

> Seeing and hearing what others can achieve often inspires children.

Learning to compete In society there is no getting away from competition – think of how many competitive situations you face in any day. Given that the world of music is highly competitive, it may be no bad thing to get young performers accustomed to competing, particularly if they want to become professionals. Even if they do not, children will encounter competitiveness in all walks of life, and need the ability to recognize and deal with it. Entering music festivals is as good a way as any to acquire this.

Confidence to persevere Winning a competition can have a real effect on a child's playing career. Success gives young players confidence, making them more inclined to take on new challenges in the future. If they develop a taste for competitions (as many do), there are plenty to enter – and each success may be not only something to celebrate in itself but also a step towards a career as a professional musician.

Teamwork Many festivals also offer group and ensemble classes. This means that children who are members of choirs, chamber ensembles, groups and bands can also benefit from the opportunity to display their musical skills, working and performing with others – and from the adjudicator's useful feedback and advice. Normally it is the conductor or director who will enter the group for the competition, but older children who run their own groups may feel confident to enter themselves if there is an appropriate class. When a group rehearses with a competition in mind – either with or without tuition – rehearsals are likely to be more focused than usual.

Constructive and impartial feedback In most festivals, adjudicators deliver their comments at the end of each class. Good judges are highly skilled in encouraging and inspiring young musicians, and many performers – whether they win a prize or not – are highly motivated by the combination of performing in public, hearing others play, and having the reaction of a wise adjudicator. Since the adjudicator is likely to be unfamiliar to the performer, his or her words may have more immediate impact than those of a parent or teacher. In addition, a judge may have a different perspective, which may happen to unravel a long-standing difficulty; it is also likely that adjudicators will reinforce points repeatedly made by teachers.

Good competition judges are
highly skilled in encouraging and
inspiring young musicians.

For the teacher, a pupil's festival performance can be a rare occasion to sit back and listen objectively to the results of weeks, or even months, of preparation. This can reveal many things that may not be immediately apparent during lessons – how the pupil responds to performing in public, for example, which is not always predictable.

The drawbacks of festivals and competitions

Any form of competition has its drawbacks, because of course not everybody can win. The fact that these events usually take place in front of an audience can intensify the pressure of competing – and therefore failure to be among the winners can be both upsetting and demoralizing.

Many teachers and parents argue that festivals and competitions represent a form of competitiveness that is incompatible with artistic expression and creative music-making. Some claim that competition destroys the joy of making music, and feel that it is better to protect children – particularly young children – from too much pressure and competitiveness. Additionally, though the result may tell you something about your child's ability, it will also reflect and be influenced by many other factors: the other competitors, the adjudicator's personal taste and preferences, the acoustics of the venue, or any number of other unpredictable or unforeseeable factors. This is true for the winners and losers alike.

Winning and losing – coping with competition

There are plenty of ways to maximize the benefits of competitions while minimizing the disadvantages. Firstly, it is important to make sure that you, your child and your child's teacher are all happy for your child to take part. Once again, this is a matter of finding out what will be involved, and providing your child with as much information as possible. Many young children will be happy to perform, seemingly without nerves, simply because they are naturally confident and have not yet learned to be anxious. If this is the case, you may find that the confidence they gain from performing will carry them through to the later years and higher stages of competition. Some older children may feel more anxious in a competitive environment, or uncomfortable about performing in public: if this is the case, be reassuring and allow them to make the final decision. Children need to know that parental love and support doesn't depend on the outcome of a competition or exam.

Children need to know that parental love and support doesn't depend on the outcome of a competition or exam.

A few other important points are worth bearing in mind and, if necessary, passing on to your child. The well-worn phrase 'it's not the winning, it's the taking part that counts' is still a wise principle! The main object of these events is to make music in front of an appreciative audience. You may also point out that the result is normally just one person's opinion of one particular performance. Also, older children in particular may understand that comparison with other performers has limited significance and it's the comparison with their own best that is useful. You could argue that in this way, as long as effort is being put in, no child is really ever a loser. These points help in two ways: they not only take the sting out of losing and guard against disappointment but also help children to understand that winning, while valuable, is not all-important. (It is essential to present these ideas *before* a competition rather than resorting to them after a disappointing result.)

The main object of these events is to make music in front of an appreciative audience.

Music-making is not a sport and it is very difficult to justify a 'first-past-the-post' approach in assessing it. Many organizers of festivals and competitions realize that 'winning' and 'losing' at music are artificial concepts, and in many music festivals around the world there has been a move towards a less competitive ethos, with gradings such as 'outstanding', 'very good', 'promising' and 'insecure' instead of simple marks. Sympathetic and intelligent adjudicators know how to handle the situation so that everyone enjoys and learns from the experience and the risks of demoralization are minimized.

After the event, try to celebrate your child's achievement, whatever the result. Children often want to do well to please their parents. It is important, therefore, that you do not show disappointment if your child does not do as well as you may have expected or hoped. If a performance isn't a success, your child will usually be perfectly aware of this. Try not to add to the disappointment by criticizing. It is the teacher's job to look constructively at how things might be improved next time, so that the pupil still benefits from the experience.

After the event, try to celebrate your child's achievement, whatever the result.

High-profile competitions

Events that receive radio or television coverage put competitions into a new league again. Many of the organizing committees of these competitions are very aware of the various psychological problems that participants may have to deal with – from the elation yet potential confusion and turmoil of winning to the damage that disappointment might bring. Entrants can therefore expect to be treated with a certain degree of care and attention.

Unlike competitive festivals, which are primarily aimed at amateurs, these competitions are generally intended for those who hope to become professional. In the case of the former, it is most likely that the impetus for entering will come from the teacher (or possibly the parent). In the case of advanced competitions, however, it should be the participants themselves who make the decision to enter – so it will be very important to discuss at length the purpose of entering and to have realistic expectations.

Whatever the result, young performers can expect to benefit in several ways. In the course of a competition they will meet other highly skilled musicians, sometimes from all over the country (even all over the world), including professional musicians – performers, teachers and critics – who will provide help, advice and support; they will have the opportunity to perform in major venues to large, interested audiences; and they may receive a great deal of media attention. Many of these competitions now include additional supportive activities like workshops and masterclasses (in which well-known professionals give public lessons). These both lessen the competitive element and bring the event more into focus with contemporary educational thinking – making the whole experience much more valuable.

Key points

- Festivals and competitions can really motivate a child, giving a focus and purpose to lessons and practice.
- Competitive performance may suit your child and be good preparation for a competitive world, but never force a child to take part.
- Finding out practical details of the event well in advance will help to reduce stress and increase enjoyment.
- Taking part truly is more important than winning – there are many benefits for all competitors.
- As long as it is the joy of music-making that is kept uppermost in the mind, entering music festivals or competitions, big or small, will always be worthwhile.

Chapter 16

STAYING ON TRACK

Parents want the best for their children. Where music is concerned, the best that we can wish for is that young pupils receive effective teaching which enables them to have enjoyable, rewarding musical experiences outside lessons. Ideally this will inspire them to continue making music all their lives.

For this to happen, children need to be motivated – to feel that making music is of value to them. They also need to make progress – to know that they are improving as musicians. Motivation and progress are linked (a motivated child will usually make progress, and progress motivates a child to continue), but both are fragile and easily damaged by a range of problems. This is particularly true once the novelty of the initial stages of learning has worn off.

Learning an instrument is a long haul and needs careful management. Therefore, in order to protect your child's music-making at this formative stage, it helps if you understand motivation and progress, and know how to deal with any problems that may arise.

Motivation

There are two kinds of motivation. Extrinsic motivation has an external source and may come from a good result in an exam or a concert success, perhaps, or from receiving high praise. Intrinsic motivation, on the other hand, comes from a person's inner desire to do well with music and enjoy it for its own sake. Children who develop this type of motivation will probably make better progress.

Most people experience both types, often at the same time. They also move from one to the other. For example, it is natural for a child to be extrinsically motivated before a competition – to anticipate the prize, status and praise that may come from winning. But at other times he or she may make music for the sheer joy of doing so – not for any external reason, but because in itself it is emotionally fulfilling or intellectually stimulating. This indicates that your child is developing intrinsic motivation.

Once you feel that your child is positively motivated, it is essential to maintain that motivation at the highest levels possible. You can help by making sure that musical tasks (such as learning a new piece or mastering a difficult scale) are always completed, and to the best of your child's ability. This leads to confidence, which in turn will motivate a child towards the next challenge. In addition, make sure goals are realistic. Good teachers always try to present their pupils with tasks that are challenging but achievable, because meeting a challenge helps a child's confidence and motivation to grow. Therefore if you or your child has a particular goal in mind (passing a particular exam, for example), check with the teacher that there is a reasonable chance of success, as failure can drain motivation.

Goals create motivation, but they need to be realistic.

Try also to ensure that your child always has a variety of challenges – exams, festivals, public performances, new musical experiences, and learning a broad range of music. In this way, interest is maintained and there is always something exciting to anticipate. (See Chapter 9 for other practical ways in which you can help keep your child motivated.)

Progress

Understanding and measuring progress is not straightforward. No two children develop as musicians at the same rate, so it is rarely useful to compare the progress of one child with another. Even children of similar ages have different skills and abilities, which are in turn dependent on many factors. (Chapter 9 looks at helpful ways of thinking about progress, particularly for beginners.)

111

With good teaching and plenty of practice, your child's playing will be improving. There will almost certainly be times when you will notice fast, furious and obvious progress – in the very early stages of learning, for example. But at other times it will appear to be much slower. Weeks (or sometimes months) may go by during which no discernible progress seems to take place. This is very much in the nature of learning a musical instrument – all children will reach a plateau from time to time – and it may take a while before you observe progress again. Be very patient and supportive during these periods: they will pass. Parents can help by praising every success, however minor, and by sharing their children's pleasure in any achieve-ment they feel that they have made. Once again, encourage a range of musical activities so that your child always has something of interest to look forward to.

Sometimes progress will be very obvious – at others it will appear to be slow. This is normal.

In order to be motivated your child will need to feel that he or she is improving as a musician. The proof of this achievement may be passing exams or winning competitions, but it should be remembered that these are just outward signs of progress: a child may gain just as much motivation, pleasure and reward from less obvious things – mastering a difficult piece, writing a song, performing in public, discovering a new style of music, or making a technical breakthrough.

How to tell if something is wrong

Don't go looking for problems! All children have ups and downs with their music, just as they do with any other activity. From time to time they may experience minor frustrations, and they will no doubt find some aspects of music training more rewarding than others. But most children cope with these little setbacks and you should simply try to be supportive, listening sympathetically to any grumbles. If you can help practically, do so with as little fuss as possible; if you can't, be reassured that many small problems resolve themselves quickly. Keep an eye on the situation, but very often an issue will either sort itself out or be quickly forgotten about.

However there is always the chance that your child could be having more significant difficulties. There may be a loss of interest in playing, or a reluctance (even refusal) to practise, go to lessons or attend rehearsals for band or orchestra. Motivational strategies may stop working. Sometimes a teacher will perceive that something is wrong and tell you that your child is making slower progress than usual or seems uninterested (or worse, distressed) during lessons. Your child may not tell you directly that something is wrong: many children don't feel able to describe their problems or may be overtaken by the silence of adolescence; others are reluctant to worry their parents, or don't want to seem ungrateful for lessons or opportunities. But you may have an instinct that things aren't quite right, in which case some detective work might be needed.

Careful questioning will usually help you to find out what is wrong. Avoid overly direct or leading questions – the most effective will be those that stimulate conversation. 'What part of your music lessons do you enjoy most (or least)?', for example, will encourage your child to reflect and explain. Ask gently and sensitively, and choose your moment carefully, to prevent your child feeling pressured. Be sympathetic, understanding and supportive in any ensuing discussion. Allow your child to make his or her case and, together, try to find a solution. You may also need to find an explanation from someone else, such as the instrumental teacher, or possibly a class teacher at school – anyone who might be able to shed light on the situation. If you suspect that the problem is serious or highly sensitive, avoid confrontation or even discussion until you have a clearer idea of what it might be.

If there is a problem, allow your child to make his or her case and, together, try to find a solution.

The main areas in which problems may arise are listed below, together with some advice about identifying and solving them:

- instrument trouble
- teacher trouble
- child protection issues
- boredom
- workload
- social difficulties
- burn-out
- parental expectations

Instrument trouble There are two types of instrument trouble. The first happens when your child feels that he or she is learning the 'wrong' instrument altogether and now wants to change to something else. The instrument may be physically uncomfortable, or unsuitable for the preferred style of music; it may not offer sufficient opportunities for performance. The instrument may simply be no longer liked! Your child may be reluctant to tell you any of this, feeling perhaps that it is too late to change, or that it's somehow disloyal to the teacher, the instrument, or even the parent who purchased it.

The truth is that learning any instrument is never wasted, because as well as acquiring specific technical skills, a child develops a general musical competence that can usually be transferred to another instrument. Starting a second instrument is much easier than the first – for both child and parent. Your child will already have jumped many of the necessary hurdles: even seemingly unrelated instruments use the same notation system, the same way of counting and thinking about music and even similar techniques. And if changing instrument brings about a new interest in music, this can only be a good thing. In addition, taking up a second instrument doesn't mean that the first must be dropped – many children happily learn two or even three instruments and gain from doing so. But the choice of the second instrument must be made with care. Encourage your child to think about some of the issues discussed earlier in this book in relation to choosing an instrument (see Chapters 4 and 5), and consult teachers and other players.

113

> **If changing instrument brings about a new interest in music, this can only be a good thing.**

Some reasons for changing instrument may seem more sensible than others. If, for example, a popular child at school plays the trumpet and your child wants to gain popularity by playing it too, it may instead be an idea to try to renew your child's enthusiasm for his or her own instrument. Give a reminder of *its* possibilities by finding recordings of talented performers, or going to concerts where the instrument is featured. Even learning pieces in a new style can remind young players of the potential and versatility of their chosen instrument.

The second type of instrument trouble is when your child is happy with the choice of instrument but may have a problem with the way it is set up. A violin, for example, may have a poorly adjusted bridge or incorrectly positioned soundpost; or a clarinet mouthpiece may be the wrong shape for your child's particular dental structure, or its reeds of the wrong strength. These problems could cause anything from intense frustration to physical pain. While most teachers are excellent at spotting them, sometimes they can go undetected. Children (especially young ones) may not be able to describe physical sensations accurately; or they may not realize that a particular sensation or discomfort signifies a problem with their instrument (simply assuming that the fault lies in their playing). Look out for clues indicating that your child finds playing difficult or disagreeable. It can be worth gently asking if anything feels uncomfortable – or asking the teacher to look out for signs.

Solutions here can be very simple. Minor alterations to the way an instrument is set up or small mechanical repairs (consult a specialist repairer) may make all the difference. A change – advised by the teacher – to the way in which the pupil stands, sits or holds the instrument may help. Another solution may be changing to a new model – one that is easier to play, lighter, louder, smaller, larger. Your child may simply not like the sound the instrument makes, so changing it for one of better quality may be a real source of motivation. As children progress, they tend to need better instruments in any case: buying a new one for your child is a sign that you recognize and value his or her music-making.

As children progress, they tend to need better instruments.

Singers, too, can have trouble with their 'instrument'. Changes in the voice occur around adolescence. These are often dramatic in boys, but can affect some girls too: the voice can become unpredictable and hard to manage. A good teacher will know how to help your child cope with this, but as a parent you need to be both patient and supportive.

Teacher trouble A good relationship with the teacher is vital – entertaining and enjoyable lessons are a sound basis for learning. It is important, though, that your child is getting the most out of lessons, and any lack of motivation or progress – or anxiety about or reluctance to go to lessons – may well indicate that the teacher isn't getting the best from your child.

The relationship between teacher and pupil can be intense. This tends to inspire and motivate children, but it also needs careful handling. Children generally want to please their teachers and become anxious or distressed if they feel they can't – if the teacher appears annoyed or impatient. Good teachers would never intentionally upset a pupil, and yet a simple misunderstanding can easily get blown out of proportion. And a pupil–teacher relationship might be fine for years, but change when the child reaches adolescence and suddenly acquires a different set of attitudes and priorities. Your child might develop tastes in music which the teacher doesn't share, or may want to learn skills that the teacher doesn't feel qualified to teach. They might have dif - ferent aims: your child may want to take exams that the teacher doesn't feel are appropriate. Good teachers modify their teaching to suit each pupil, but sometimes compromise is difficult.

It can be hard to know what to do if, for any of these reasons, you feel dissatisfied with your child's teacher. Simple misunderstandings – or differences of opinion or approach – can usually be sorted out by talking. Depending on your child's age and the problem in question, it may be best if your child talks to the teacher. But you may need to do this on your child's behalf, or at least be present at the discussion. Don't be afraid to say what is on your mind, but do so without confrontation. A sensitive teacher will address your concerns and it is likely that, given time and effective communication, things will improve. Even structuring the lesson in a new way or choosing different pieces can make a noticeable improvement to your child's motivation.

115

If after a while you see no improvement – and your child is still demoralized – you may need to change teacher. This is not a decision to take lightly. Children can become very attached to their teachers, and may not appreciate that it is in their best interests to move on. You too may feel a degree of loyalty and would not wish to hurt the teacher's feelings. It is often easier to stay with a person and a routine that you know! And yet a different teaching style, different priorities or simply a different personality can revitalize your child's playing. This is particularly true for children who have been learning with the same teacher for a long time. A good teacher, recognizing the problem, may be the one to suggest that the pupil moves on elsewhere. (This may happen even when your child is happy and settled, if the teacher feels your child needs more specialized attention at a more advanced level.)

The transition to a new teacher should be as smooth as possible. To avoid leaving your child with no lessons at all, make sure that you have a new teacher lined up before you give notice to the old one. This isn't always easy, as some teachers are in great demand and may have no vacancies. If you have a particular teacher in mind, try to arrange a trial lesson first.

The transition to a new teacher should be as smooth as possible.

The change need not be from one individual teacher to another: your child might respond well to a different type of lesson for a while. For example, a child who has had one-to-one teaching might benefit from a period of group lessons (see Chapter 6); or a teacher using the Suzuki method may help a child who lacks confidence in memory work. For practical reasons it may be better for your child to have instrumental lessons and band or orchestra on the same day and in the same place (a Saturday music centre, for example). And changing teachers is often necessary when a child moves house or changes school. If pupil and teacher have had a very good relationship, parting will have to be handled with particular care.

Whatever the reason for change, it needs to be managed sensitively. Try to discuss the possibility of change with your child at an early stage. Explain the reasons for the change, and its advantages, but allow him or her to express any reservations or misgivings. Most teachers are very understanding and are used to losing pupils and gaining new ones – but give as much notice as you can. You may feel it is a good idea to coordinate a change of teacher with other changes – with a move from primary to secondary school, for example. Conversely, you may feel that too much change at once may be damaging, and prefer to make the change at a time when everything else is settled.

Child protection issues Occasionally you may meet a more complex problem. Children have a right to be treated with care and respect – and you can expect that teachers will treat your child in this way. If your child is taking part in group activities you can also expect that the teacher will make sure that everyone treats each other appropriately. Parents might wish to check that their children are aware of these rights – perhaps by saying that no one has the right to hurt them or do anything to them that makes them feel uncomfortable. In general teachers are committed and caring, and many are trained in matters of child protection. Many music organizations and individual teachers have a code of behaviour to ensure that children can learn in an environment free from danger, bullying, racism, and emotional, physical or sexual abuse; and instances of these things are extremely rare indeed.

If your child is repeatedly uncomfortable, frightened or distressed at the prospect of a music lesson, you will need to discover why. Calmly encourage your child to speak about the matter, and listen very carefully to what he or she says. Here it will be important not to ask questions that seem to suggest particular answers. You may want to make a note of what your child has said. If you feel that there is a problem which should be pursued, do so with great care. Your child must know that you will deal with the matter sensibly: don't promise to keep secrets, and explain early on that you may need to share this information with others.

If the problem seems to be your child's mistreatment at the hands of another pupil or group member, do not confront this other child or the parents directly. Find out who among the teaching staff deals with child protection and arrange a private meeting (without your child, at first) to raise the issue. There will normally be a procedure for dealing with problems of bullying and abuse.

If you discover that it is the teacher who may be treating your child inappropriately it is extremely unwise to confront the teacher directly. Neither should you talk to other pupils or their parents, as this spreads rumours that may well be untrue. In this instance, it is advisable to contact an organization who will have the resources to deal with this in a confidential, sensitive manner. In the UK this is likely to be the NSPCC, social services, or the police child protection group.

Boredom Good teachers provide a range of activities and teach in an imaginative and engaging way, continually challenging their pupils and tapping into their particular interests, so maintaining motivation. The chemistry doesn't always work, however, and this can lead to boredom on the child's part. (In 2000, a survey by ABRSM attempted to discover why children give up music-making. The results showed that the greatest number of pupils – a third of all those who had stopped taking lessons – gave up simply because they became bored.)

In some cases it may be that the teacher is no longer appropriate for your child. Children's abilities and tastes develop and change as they grow older, and a fresh approach, as mentioned above, may be the answer to a waning interest. Or the teacher can, with your help, learn more about your child's musical tastes, and find activities and pieces that better match them. You can also avoid boredom setting in by encouraging your child to take part in social music-making activities. This may be a band, orchestra or other smaller group; pianists can play duets or accompany friends. As well as being fun, this will put their music-making into a wider context.

Workload Many children find that their music-making takes up a lot of time and that this causes conflict with schoolwork and other activities. Not having enough time can cause stress in young people and may demotivate them. In addition, progress may slow down if practice time is squeezed by too many other activities. You can help by encouraging your child to organize his or her time carefully. Finding extra time for practice is normally solved if you can persuade your child to get up a little earlier in the morning. Some children feel that they want to do everything all at once, which can cause time-management problems. Ask your child to consider whether some activities can wait – perhaps until the school holidays. Try to even out the balance between activities that need constant practice and attention – like music – and others that can wait for periods when time is less precious.

You can help by encouraging your child to organize his or her time carefully.

There will be times when schoolwork has to take priority – exam periods, for example – and you should be aware of these (as should your child's instrumental teacher). To make space for revision you and your child may feel it is sensible to relax the lesson or practising schedule or reduce the amount of music-making. But stopping playing during these periods is rarely a good idea. Apart from the clear benefits that instrumental work has for brain function, taking part in any sort of music-making activity keeps the mind alert and fresh; it may act as therapy or distraction and, indirectly, impact quite significantly on the whole exam period.

Social difficulties As children grow older, they can become acutely self-conscious – it may simply not be 'cool' to play a musical instrument. If there is real pressure at school to conform, children may feel that even carrying a musical instrument makes them look too 'different'. Some children may be intimidated by peers who tease them for practising rather than socializing; leaving mainstream classes for music lessons or exams can also be a cause of friction. Be sensitive to this, as it can be a powerful demotivator (but not one that your child is likely to tell you about). The most important remedy is to give your child praise and encouragement so that he or she has the self-belief to continue being 'different'.

Praise and encouragement will give your child self-belief.

Children often find that there is strength in numbers – so a group carrying instruments on the school bus may feel special rather than intimidated. Encourage your child to make music outside school so that the interest takes on a life of its own.

Burn-out Some children simply burn out – in other words, they become tired and disillusioned with music and want to stop. This can happen for several reasons. Starting very young may be a factor: some children, by the age of seven or eight, may have been learning for as many as four years – during which time their interests and needs will have changed hugely. You will therefore need to take particular care to keep your child suitably motivated and challenged.

Other children may react badly to what they perceive as too much pressure – from parents, from the teacher, or from school. Your child may be reluctant to tell you if this is the case, as he or she may not want to cause trouble or seem ungrateful for opportunities. But if he or she seems to have lost motivation, you need to ask whether too much pressure might be the cause. If so, motivation may return when adults involved back off slightly, giving the pupil some space to proceed at his or her own pace.

Motivation may return when adults involved back off slightly.

Another reason for burn-out may be that your child has had a particularly intense period of musical activity – for example preparing for an exam or a festival – and needs a change of pace or a new approach to revitalize interest. If parents monitor their child's level of enthusiasm, investigating and then acting on any decline in interest, they may be able to pre-empt early burn-out.

Parental expectations You will naturally want your child to do well, and it makes sense to seek out opportunities for music-making, to encourage and reward progress, and to have goals and targets which structure your child's learning. But this should always be in response to what your child wants. Unless he or she is happy making music for its own sake, your encouragement simply becomes pressure. Pressure, especially a lot of it, has a negative effect, turning music-making into a duty or a chore. The child's natural reaction will be to lose motivation, and maybe to want to give up. So consider your child's aims first, not yours. Ask what he or she wants from music – a career, a leisure activity, or opportunities for socializing? If your expectations are realistic and based firmly on what your child wants, you will be able to determine how to adapt the music education 'package' to suit your child's needs.

119

Too much pressure can turn music-making into a duty or a chore.

Finding the right balance between encouragement and pressure can be difficult. Insisting on a certain amount of practice each week means that your child will gain more from lessons – and in the early stages at least this may well propel your child to higher levels of achievement where music-making is more enjoyable. Yet insisting that children continue to learn a particular instrument against their will, when it has become onerous to them, helps nobody.

My child is determined to give up!
If your child suddenly announces that he or she wants to give up learning an instrument, try to find out why. Sometimes this desire is an over-reaction to one or several of the difficulties outlined earlier in this chapter, so it is important to ask your child to explain to you the reasons behind his or her decision before agreeing to stop lessons altogether. There may be a simple solution. If, for example, a child dislikes the pieces or style of music that he or she is currently learning, a change of repertoire might make all the difference. Alternatively, some gentle negotiation may help. A compromise might lead to a surprisingly positive outcome. For example, you might suggest that your

child waits to give up until he or she has played at a particular concert or festival. The applause and general lifting of spirits at the event might make him or her want to carry on after all.

If your child really is determined to give up, and attempts to renew his or her interest are unsuccessful, there is not much you can do. While in the future your child may regret the decision, forcing him or her to continue will only produce frustration and bad feeling. If you and your child do decide to stop lessons, give the teacher as much notice as possible (the teacher's contract may specify a notice period). A good teacher will manage the concluding lessons carefully and try to give the pupil a positive memory of music lessons. You may feel disappointed or frustrated, but try not to pass these feelings on to your child; he or she may learn to associate music with arguments or conflict and be unlikely to return to it with any pleasure in the future. Manage the situation carefully, and you may leave the door open for further musical activity later on.

Key points

- A child needs motivation to make progress; progress leads to more motivation.
- Motivation can be damaged by a range of problems – be aware of the risks.
- Don't go looking for problems, as most difficulties are minor and temporary.
- Listen to your child and take notice if there really does seem to be a problem.
- If possible, investigate difficulties and do everything you can to encourage a child to continue.
- If your child really is determined to give up, do not cause frustration and bad feeling by refusing to allow this.

Chapter 17

MUSIC FOR CHILDREN WITH SPECIAL NEEDS

Music enables people to communicate, create and participate, and is a powerful source of self-esteem; it is often profoundly beneficial to children with special needs, so helping them to gain access to music-making of one sort or another is important. This chapter looks at different types of music-making for children with special needs, and also at the ways in which music may help with some specific difficulties. It is intended only as an introduction to this specialized area and cannot help you to recognize or diagnose a particular condition. If you suspect your child has special needs, it is important to raise this with his or her school or with a health-care professional. If your child does have special needs, you may already be receiving assistance from health workers, educational practitioners or social services. These people should be able to give you more specific advice about music provision for your child – about obtaining help and guidance from trained music therapists or other suitably qualified teachers.

Music is often profoundly beneficial to children with special needs.

Approaches to music teaching and learning for different types of special needs

Many children with special needs are able to take part in mainstream musical activities, and education and examination authorities often take great care to provide equal access to teaching and assessment. Some children – those with severe physical or mental disabilities, or learning or behavioural difficulties – may not find it possible to participate in the same way. Yet music therapy (see below) can be of great help, allowing music still to be a vital part of their lives. Some children may benefit from both approaches, and many move towards mainstream participation after a period of more therapeutic and remedial music-making.

Every child will have different tastes, requirements and aspirations regarding music, and, as with all children, those with special needs should have, as far as possible, a choice in the kind of music-making they undertake. Your child may find certain instruments or types of music-making more rewarding than others, and it is important to be sensitive to this. You should also consider whether a particular approach to teaching and learning is appropriate for your child's needs. For example, a wide range of conditions can make reading and understanding difficult for children. Some with reading difficulties cope perfectly well with music notation, but others will be less comfortable with it. Notation is however only one of many ways into music. Certain methods of teaching and plenty of musical styles – such as jazz, folk or pop – rely less heavily on notation and may allow your child easier access to the pleasures and benefits of music-making.

Consider whether a particular approach to teaching and learning is appropriate for your child's needs.

This chapter now looks at some of the more common conditions (listed below), together with particular issues to consider and suggestions on how to get the most out of music-making.

- autistic spectrum disorders (ASDs)
- behavioural, emotional and social difficulties (BESDs)
- Down's syndrome
- dyslexia
- dyspraxia
- hearing impairment
- physical disability
- visual impairment

Autistic spectrum disorders (ASDs) People with autistic spectrum disorders – such as childhood autism and Asperger syndrome – have varying degrees of impairment in social communication, social understanding and imagination. They may also be extremely averse to change and feel compelled to follow routines. Communication difficulties can make access to learning more difficult; problems with social understanding may make it hard for a child to join in with a group; and difficulty imagining or conceptualizing can lead to problems in processing written or spoken information and turning it into music. Additionally, many people with ASDs hear and absorb music differently (they may even find certain sounds unbearable). Yet they often have particular musical abilities, such as absolute pitch or a highly developed memory for music. It is important to use and develop these strengths.

With severe autism, music therapy can be effective in helping children to communicate, acquire self-esteem and develop social skills like listening to others, sharing and taking turns. Many children with an ASD respond more readily to singing than they do to speaking, so teachers and therapists incorporate music into the daily routine to improve memory and concentration.

Others may benefit from more mainstream music teaching, perhaps with certain modifications. For example, children who have difficulty settling in group situations may find this easier when music-making is the shared activity – so long as the goals are made very clear at the outset.

Children with an ASD may need their lessons to follow the same strict routine each week: they may become distressed or anxious otherwise. (Imaginative teaching in which lesson structure is varied may be unsuitable for a child with an ASD.) Many children with ASDs find it easier to learn by imitation, so may be uncomfortable if teachers use too many words or explain things imprecisely. Activities without precise directions or predictable outcomes (such as improvisation) may need careful handling because they rely less on 'rules' and more on ideas. Yet because music is primarily a non-verbal means of communication, it can help children with ASDs to express themselves, their ideas and emotions without necessarily having to use words.

Because music is primarily a non-verbal means of communication, it can help children with ASDs to express themselves.

Behavioural, emotional and social difficulties (BESDs) There are many causes of behavioural, emotional and social difficulties, and many symptoms too – music can help in a variety of ways. Conditions such as attention deficit hyperactivity disorder (ADHD) may mean that a child has a poor attention span. An experienced teacher will find ways of varying music activities so that lessons remain interesting and can stimulate for longer periods. Certain instruments may be better than others for engaging and maintaining a child's interest – namely those on which a sound can be produced readily and easily, such as piano, keyboard, guitar or percussion. If you are helping a child with ADHD to choose an instrument, it is sensible to try several. By choosing their instrument for themselves, children will feel more committed and have a stronger sense of ownership.

123

For some children with BESDs, taking part in a music group helps them to modify their behaviour, because they learn that they have to cooperate with others in order to achieve the desired musical result. And the other children in the group are more likely to be helpful and tolerant of difference as they focus on a common musical goal. Children with emotional difficulties often find that music is one of the few ways in which they can express themselves and their anxieties and problems. Music therapy can also be a very powerful tool here.

For some children with BESDs, taking part in a music group helps them to modify their behaviour.

Down's syndrome The delay in certain aspects of physical and intellectual development caused by Down's syndrome can result in a range of difficulties. These include impaired motor skills, making use of the hands and fingers for small movements such as those necessary to play some musical instruments more difficult. For this reason, children with Down's syndrome may find it easier to play an instrument that can produce sound without complicated movements of the hands, fingers or mouth – the piano or electronic keyboard, for example, or certain types of percussion. Learning to speak and acquiring vocabulary may also be difficult, and they may have short-term memory problems. An experienced teacher will break ideas and concepts down into small, manageable units.

Poor muscle tone is another problem, and this can affect posture, which in turn may make breathing more difficult. For some children this may be helped by singing, or playing a wind instrument.

Down's syndrome may also cause hearing difficulties and ear infections, and yet many children with Down's syndrome have excellent listening skills, and can more easily reproduce music from memory (sometimes after hearing it only briefly) than they can by reading notation. This can be of great benefit in developing creative music-making.

Dyslexia People with dyslexia find it hard to make links between written information and ideas and concepts. This can affect their ability to read and write, to memorize and to organize their thoughts. Yet children with dyslexia are often extremely imaginative and creative, with a good ear for music, and – if carefully taught – they can be highly successful in every area of musical activity.

If carefully taught, children with dyslexia can be highly successful in every area of musical activity.

Teaching will have to be particularly methodical and imaginative, and is often most successful when directed more to creative activities like improvisation and composition. For children with dyslexia, instruments that require the reading of more than one line of music at a time (such as the piano) may be more difficult than those that use just one line (such as string or wind instruments). However, many children with dyslexia do very well as pianists, so don't be put off if your child is determined. Standard music notation may present reading challenges, but it is possible to find teachers highly skilled in helping people with dyslexia to overcome this; educational and examination bodies often make special arrangements too. Dyslexia can affect a child's ability to translate instructions on the page into physical movements on an instrument, so a mechanically complex instrument may not be suitable. The most natural instrument of all – the voice – may be ideal for children with dyslexia.

When choosing an instrument, try to consult a music teacher with experience of the condition. Many music teachers are now familiar with the issues involved in teaching children with dyslexia, and will have a number of different approaches and strategies to help pupils. These include special techniques to aid memorization of note names, fingerings and rhythmic patterns, as well as careful testing and monitoring of the pupil's ability to read and understand music. As with all good teaching, singing from notation should always play a part in the lesson, since this helps pupils with dyslexia to translate notation into physical movement, and it also aids general reading skills.

Dyspraxia Children with dyspraxia – a condition affecting the ability to control movement – may also have a short concentration span and take longer than others to respond to instructions. In addition, they can find it difficult to retain information or organize themselves and their environment. As a result they may be shy and anxious, and have communication difficulties. Learning an instrument or singing will help to develop motor skills, aid relaxation, build confidence, and improve posture and breathing.

Certain instruments may be more suitable than others – particularly those that are easy to control. If possible, take advice from teachers with experience of teaching children with dyspraxia, as they will have a number of techniques to help pupils. They understand that children should not have too many tasks to do at once. Skills, concepts or new pieces of information are broken down into the smallest units possible and patiently reinforced many times. They allow the pupil plenty of time to complete a task, or to grasp fully any new ideas, and may reinforce the learning of specific movements by directing the pupil's arms or hands. There also need to be strategies in place to compensate for any poor memory or lack of organizational skills – for example, it will help if the teacher uses the pupil's notebook to indicate very clearly indeed exactly what and how the child should practise.

125

Hearing impairment Skill in music isn't entirely based on the ability to hear, and there are several professional musicians who are profoundly deaf. A hearing impairment should not therefore prevent your child from making music. Even profoundly deaf children are very sensitive to the effects of sound – especially vibration, which they can feel through the body by touching instruments or loudspeakers. Of course, those who have limited hearing may need to approach music slightly differently. For example, hearing-impaired listeners may have difficulty with very complex or ornate styles of music that contain many different sounds at once; something with a strong, constant rhythm is likely to be easier to hear and feel.

A hearing impairment should not prevent your child from making music.

Choosing the right instrument can be crucial. Instruments well worth considering are those that allow the player to feel vibrations directly as well as hear the sounds: these include the guitar (because it is held against the body) or the harp (because the strings are close to the ears). Depending on the impairment, instruments which make low sounds – such as the bass clarinet, tenor and baritone saxophone, or electric bass guitar – may be easier to hear. The cello and double bass, both of which make a low sound and are held against the body, may be appropriate too, but will best suit those with mild or moderate deficiencies. More severely impaired players may find them problematic because it can be difficult to hear whether or not notes are in tune.

Brass instruments can be suitable if the player learns to distinguish pitches by feeling their different vibrations through the bell. Percussion instruments can be felt and heard through 'sympathetic' vibrations. Vibrations can be felt, for example, via the floor, the stand on which the instrument is held, or simply by being near the instrument. Severely impaired students may feel vibrations by wrapping their legs around a bongo or conga drum.

Experienced teachers will try to eliminate all background noise during lessons, and they may develop particular ways of communicating with the pupil if speech is a problem. While music-making with other children shouldn't be too problematic for hearing-impaired pupils, they may find it difficult to understand the teacher if they are placed too far away to lip-read the teacher's speech. In this case, they may need a hearing student to help them.

Physical disability Children with physical disabilities are likely to be challenged mainly by their choice of instrument. If standing is a problem, there are many instruments that are (or can be) played in a normal sitting position, such as piano or keyboard, most woodwind and brass instruments, and some string instruments (violin, viola and guitar). Other instruments that demand a particular posture while sitting – the cello for example – may be more difficult. For those with restricted hand use, a brass instrument may be suitable because the sound is controlled by the mouth and lips; piano or keyboard may also be possible. Consider also the weight of the instrument – some children may find it hard to keep their instrument in the correct position for any length of time. Some instruments can be adapted to make them easier to play – and remember too that singing is an excellent form of music-making for those who cannot manage an instrument.

Visual impairment Many children with visual impairment develop enhanced hearing, listening and memory skills which can be very helpful when learning music. They can be extremely sensitive to details of sound, with an advanced ability to distinguish between notes that are in tune and those that are not. When helping a child with a visual impairment to choose an instrument, take time to identify and explain an instrument's particular features. If possible, let your child experiment with several different instruments before making a choice. Certain instruments are harder to assemble and maintain than others (see Chapter 5), so help may be needed at first.

Many visually impaired people find notation difficult to read. Resources to help here can include large-print music, music on computer disk which can be displayed in large format (and played back for memorizing), audio recordings and Braille music. Singers will be able to read Braille music and perform at the same time. This is not normally possible for instrumentalists, who tend to learn from Braille while listening to the music in order then to play from memory. Bear in mind that teachers of Braille music notation are comparatively rare.

Experienced teachers can help visually impaired pupils in different ways. For example, visually impaired children may take longer to learn how to hold an instrument, particularly if they have never seen it played. The pupil is encouraged to concentrate on how it feels to hold the instrument and to memorize the necessary posture and movements. The child must be given guidance in exploring the instrument in order to get to know its parts and to understand how it produces its sound. Once pupils are familiar with the layout of the instrument (such as the order of the keys on a keyboard) a teacher may introduce exercises to help the pupil find certain notes or keys quickly. Because much of the learning may take place from memory, pupils will benefit from frequent lessons and plenty of practice to develop their listening skills. Some teachers will encourage their pupils to analyse the structure of each piece they are learning, as this stimulates more perceptive and fluent memorization.

127

Music therapy

The primary aim of music therapy is to address the problems of people with special needs through music. Music therapists are not necessarily teachers – though some may have teaching experience – and they don't teach music in therapy sessions. When working with young people, they will use music as a means of communicating with the child, building confidence and self-esteem. They may use improvisation or explore musical instruments to develop a relationship with the child for a variety of purposes: to solve emotional and behavioural problems, to soothe physical pain, and to encourage self-expression.

WEBWORDS music + therapy + session + mytown ▼▼▼

A course of music therapy sessions may be short, to deal with a specific difficulty, or long-term, with the aim of remedying complex psychological or physiological problems. During a session, the therapist guides the child through a range of musical activities (sometimes with the help of a co-therapist or carer). The experience is unique for each child, and for each session. A therapist will encourage a child to make music with the voice and with a variety of instruments – certain instruments may be selected for their individual sound qualities and effects. Sometimes a therapist will use well-known music, and at other times will make up music specifically to suit the child – or encourage the child to make up his or her own music. Some therapists make audio recordings of sessions, allowing them to follow the development of the therapy as it proceeds.

**A music therapy experience is unique for each child,
and for each session.**

Once again, because music is non-verbal, music therapy can enable children to express themselves in ways that do not require words, and music therapists are trained to understand and interpret these forms of expression in order to understand the child. By learning to understand children's reactions to different sounds, rhythms, styles or activities, therapists learn more about the child's problems and develop further musical activities that will help to solve them. The effects of music therapy can be extremely profound and in many cases will significantly improve a child's quality of life.

**Music therapy can enable children to express themselves
in ways that do not require words.**

> **Key points**
>
> - No one need be excluded from the joys of music-making.
> - Music can have profound benefits for children with special needs, boosting confidence, improving skills and enhancing creativity.
> - If your child has special needs ask his or her health-care provider, teacher or social worker about music-making opportunities.
> - Music therapy can be very effective, particularly for those with severe problems.

Chapter 18

THE EXCEPTIONALLY TALENTED CHILD

Some children have a particular talent for music. This can become apparent in different ways, some of them more obvious than others. If your child does seem to be unusually talented, you will need to consider how to help him or her develop this ability and achieve maximum potential. This chapter looks at how to identify whether your child is musically gifted, and what the options are for such children.

Identifying a musically talented child

A number of general characteristics and conditions seem to be peculiar to all highly talented children. They are not specific to music, but apply to a wide range of activities and disciplines and will be found in different proportions from one child to the next. Usually, highly talented children will be:

- imaginative and creative
- bright (though not necessarily intellectually outstanding)
- able to focus on one task for a considerable time (sometimes to the point of obsession)
- highly motivated, persistent, self-disciplined and committed
- full of energy and enthusiasm

Highly talented young musicians also display a number of specific musical skills which will be noticeably more developed and advanced than in other children of a similar age. If you are not a musician yourself you may not recognize them immediately, but the teacher will certainly be able to help in identifying them. These skills are:

- sense of pitch
- sense of rhythm
- psychomotor skills
- sensitivity to sound
- musical imagination
- eagerness to perform

Sense of pitch This is the ability to sing and play melodies in tune, to pick out individual notes in a chord and to remember long (and possibly complicated) tunes accurately. Children with a good sense of pitch will be able to tell whether they (or other people) are playing out of tune and will be able to correct this on their instrument. They may also have absolute or relative pitch.

Sense of rhythm This is the ability to maintain an even pulse, to sense and respond quickly to rhythmic patterns, and to memorize and repeat rhythms accurately. Children with a good sense of rhythm may find pulses and rhythmic patterns in all manner of everyday tasks. They may readily make up rhymes and raps, and may find it hard to resist responding physically to music by dancing or other bodily movement. When playing or listening to music, they will pick up tempos and tempo changes easily.

Psychomotor skills These are actions and gestures that must be consciously learned and performed but, with time and practice, become automatic as the subconscious mind absorbs them. (Tying shoelaces is a good example.) They require acute muscular coordination, with strength and agility in the fingers and hands. Children with good psychomotor skills play their instruments with little apparent effort and don't need to think too hard about the physical gestures involved. Small, controlled movements from note to note seem to be instinctive, even automatic. Away from the instrument, they may have very adept hand and finger skills (such as when typing or playing computer games).

Sensitivity to sound This is manifested in a real concern for the quality of the sound made when playing or singing. Children may spend a long time perfecting their control of tone: your child may repeat sections of music when practising, trying out different ways of playing a particular phrase or group of notes in order to get the best sound. Attention to detail in other people's live or recorded performances is another sign of this sensitivity. Some children develop a real interest in how sounds are made and how instruments work, and a number are able to identify a piece from just a few notes. (This sensitivity to sound is very useful to composers, conductors, record producers or audio engineers.)

Musical imagination Children with a highly developed musical imagination seem to have a real grasp of what they sing or play. They appear to know instinctively how to turn notes into phrases, and how to perform with a natural expressiveness. They may display an ability to understand long and complicated musical structures after reading, playing or hearing them just a few times. They may also show a marked interest or ability in composing or improvising.

Eagerness to perform This is demonstrated by a passion for performing in public, and a real confidence when doing so. Children with this have a strong sense of style and occasion – and often show few signs of nerves.

There are also, of course, many external measures of a child's talent. Pupils may achieve consistently high marks in music exams and reach the higher grades at a young age, or very quickly. They may win music competitions, do well in festivals, or become key members of a band or orchestra. Their musical abilities might be constantly in demand at school, or in local music groups. Teachers may remark on particularly rapid progress. This may be at any age: while some children display enormous talent while very small, others can take longer to 'grow into' their ability. Whatever style of music they make, truly talented children rarely go unnoticed, and music professionals will usually be happy to offer help and advice. (Although it is natural for parents to believe that their children are particularly talented, remember that prodigies are rare, and you should wait for confirmation from other specialists before getting too excited.)

Truly talented children rarely go unnoticed.

Supporting and developing a talented child

If your child has a particular talent for music and wants to develop this further, there will be many hurdles but the satisfactions will also be profound. It is essential that music-making should continue to be a source of enjoyment – and this must be the highest priority in any special arrangements that you may make.

There are a number of educational routes for musically gifted children (see 'Educational choices for talented young musicians' below) which, to different degrees, will involve changes both to your child's life and to yours. Before investigating these, consider the following questions:

- Should I make any special provision?
- What does my child want from music?
- Is this the right time?
- Am I prepared to make the commitment?

Should I make any special provision? Some parents feel that if their talented children are good enough and determined enough, they will ultimately succeed. Some also are wary of 'pushing' their children, believing that they will find their own appropriate pace without too much parental interference. It is true that many children do very well simply by attending music lessons once a week and taking part in music activities at school and elsewhere. But particularly talented children will need much more than this – extra practice time, opportunities to share their interest and make music with

131

others, opportunities to learn about all aspects of music, and the chance to broaden, develop and refine their skills to the highest levels. If you recognize this need (you will almost certainly be alerted to it by your child's teacher or the school's head of music), the possibilities of special provision need to be considered. This sometimes happens gradually – children with a real aptitude and desire for music-making will wish to seek out more and more opportunities for themselves. In giving emotional and practical support, you are already making 'special provision', and the change to a different form of music education becomes just a natural step further.

What does my child want from music? Many children are happy to have music as an absorbing hobby. They enjoy acquiring new skills on an instrument, learning new pieces, or the social side of music-making. But for some children, music becomes a fundamental part of their lives. You may notice this simply because they demand more music activities and appear to be very absorbed and committed to listening, performing and practising. Some, even at a young age, begin to talk about a career in music.

It is necessary to consider carefully the educational options here. Some parents want children to make their own educational choices and are wary of doing so on their behalf. However, children are not always fully aware of the issues involved in and possibilities offered by more specialized music teaching. Talk to your child and get as much feedback as possible before making any major decisions. Again, children should not be forced into doing something against their will. Parents of a talented child need to examine their own motives, and to make sure that all educational decisions are being taken for the child's sake – not because they want a star in the family.

Parents of a talented child need to examine their own motives.

Is this the right time? If your child displays real talent at a very young age, you will have to decide whether or not this is the right time to pursue a specialist music education. Ask musicians and musical educators to let you know about the pros and cons of specializing at a young age. It may be sensible to wait until your child is older before opting for a specialist education (thus enabling him or her to have a mainstream education first) – but your child may show such eagerness that you decide to find an educational environment where music is given high priority immediately.

Am I prepared to make the commitment? If you have reached the stage of considering special educational provision, you should also be aware of the implications for you personally. You will need to find the time and energy to take your child to lessons, courses and exams; protect practice time (which may be several hours each day); attend concerts; and generally provide support during the inevitable ups and downs. If your child does have a special talent, you will probably wish to make this high level of commitment – but it may well involve some sacrifices on your part.

There are financial considerations too – fees for schools, exams, courses, special lessons or group work; transport costs; and making sure that your child has the best instrument possible. There are many national and international trusts to help finance exceptionally talented children. A number of local authorities run scholarship schemes for young musicians, providing funds for instrumental lessons, music exams, holiday courses, instrument purchase and so on. Educational organizations, libraries and the Internet are good sources of information.

WEBWORDS trusts + musically + talented + children ▼▼▼

In the UK, the government's Music and Dance Scheme offers means-tested financial assistance to children who show exceptional potential, giving talented young musicians access to a specialist music education. The scheme provides aided places at specialist music schools, and grants for some students attending Centres for Advanced Training or junior departments of the English music conservatoires. It also supports the Choir Schools' Scholarship Scheme. (For more about these educational options see 'Educational choices for talented young musicians' on p. 133.)

WEBWORDS "Music and Dance Scheme" ▼▼▼

Practical strategies

Whether or not you know about music, there are a number of practical ways in which you can help to develop your child's ambition:

- give realistic encouragement
- support all aspects of music-making
- investigate and plan before any change

Give realistic encouragement All children need encouragement and, at the outset at least, unconditional praise for music-making is a powerful motivator for your child. You can encourage dreams – with the ambition of becoming a world-famous musician your child will clearly have the strong self-motivation to work hard – but children need also to be given realistic expectations of what they can expect to achieve with their music. As children begin to exhibit real talent, too much praise may give them an unbalanced sense of their own abilities. If children receive constant praise from you at home, they may get a shock if they find that other people's opinions of their playing are less favourable (for example those of leading experts or music college professors).

> **Children need to be given realistic expectations of what they can expect to achieve with their music.**

As your child develops as a musician, your encouragement needs to become more subtle. Always be positive, but think carefully about what you say. A talented child may know (often better than you) just how well he or she is playing, so unconsidered praise from you may start to feel meaningless. Your child may also come to resent your comments if they appear to be ill-informed. Be careful too about any criticism. In general, it is better to leave this to the teacher unless your child specifically asks you for an opinion. If you do have something critical to say, be very careful that it is expressed constructively in a way that doesn't undermine your child's confidence.

Support all aspects of music-making At home and elsewhere, all aspects of your child's music-making will need your support. Growing talent needs to be nurtured by lots of practice, so help to protect this precious time. See to it that there will be no unnecessary interruptions to a practice session by answering phone calls and fielding other distractions. Make sure that your child is developing aural skills on a regular basis, learning about the history and theory of music, and having frequent opportunities to play with others. Encourage any desire to make more music.

The more skilled children become as musicians, the more vital it is that they continue to develop both broad and deep cultural and creative interests. This will help to maintain their focus and motivation even when practice and study are hard and demanding. A musician with a broad range of tastes, interests and knowledge is likely to be a more rounded performer, so encourage any activities that will exercise and stimulate the creative mind.

134

Encourage any activities that will exercise and stimulate the creative mind.

Investigate and plan before any change If it seems that your child has exceptional talent, think carefully before making changes. Take time to consider the available options: you will not damage a talented child's development by thinking about how to proceed, but a rushed decision either way could result in problems. As well as your child's music teacher, talk to the music staff at your child's school and other musicians you know. If you decide to pursue specialist music education (see below), understand exactly what is available, and be as sure as you can be that this is what your child needs and wants. Make your child aware that entry to specialist music schools or other schemes is normally highly competitive and not all applicants are successful. (In this regard, it may be easier to adopt a 'try it and see' approach rather than making your child feel that entry to the school is the all-important focus of their musical career.)

You will not damage a talented child's development by taking time to consider how to proceed.

The role of the teacher

Exceptional students (and their parents) require much more from the teacher than technical and musical guidance. The teacher can often become a counsellor and 'life manager', advising on educational options, music activities, instruments and all other aspects of the pupil's development. If your child's skills are to be properly nurtured, you need a teacher who is capable of all this. He or she must be demanding and have high expectations – a very discerning ear is needed, along with a range of imaginative and challenging strategies to develop all aspects of your child's playing, and the ability to maintain optimum motivation. Such teachers will naturally need a deep understanding of technical matters and knowledge of a wide variety of music. They should have great reserves of patience, energy and concentration as well.

Should the teacher fit this description reasonably well, then your child is in safe hands. But different teachers have different skills and interests: some specialize in teaching beginners, some enjoy developing young players, while others prefer to work with the more talented and the more advanced. Each of these demands a different set of skills, and teachers who possess them all are extremely rare.

If your child is talented, the basic principles still apply when you are assessing a teacher's effectiveness: is the pupil happy, and motivated to keep practising and performing? Other factors come into play with gifted pupils, however. You will probably want external proof of achievement, such as particularly good marks in exams, high places in competitions and festivals, plenty of high-quality music-making with others, praise from other music professionals, and a challenging but realistic plan for a continuing music education (and, possibly, a career). Your child's teacher may well be your best ally, giving you sound advice about what is best for your child – perhaps even suggesting that he or she move to a new teacher or into a different form of music education. If you feel that the situation demands a change of teacher (for whatever reason), this needs to be handled carefully (see 'Teacher trouble' in Chapter 16).

Educational choices for talented young musicians

There are a number of different types of school and college that provide specialist music training for talented school-age musicians. Most of these organizations give pupils the time, the opportunities and the training to make music a central part of their lives. To join one of these schools, your child will be expected to show a high level of musical talent and commitment. This will usually be tested by audition and interview, but some schools also require certain academic qualifications or a particular grade of music exam to have been achieved. Although the level of competition varies, places are always sought after, and you should be prepared for failure as well as success.

Specialist music education has its advantages. Talent is nurtured in a caring and focused environment, and for highly talented musicians who may be considered 'different' and feel rather isolated in a mainstream school, a specialist school is a place in which they can flourish with like-minded and similarly able children. The school should also provide plenty of time and space to practise.

Yet there are drawbacks as well. The rather single-minded nature of such institutions may be too restricting for some pupils; others might find it dispiriting to go back to the wider world after being in such a highly charged atmosphere. And music schools can generate a culture of extreme competition because everyone is pursuing similar goals. Some children find it difficult to make the transition from mainstream school – where they may be among the very best musicians – to a specialist environment in which every pupil is highly talented; others, however, find this change highly stimulating and exciting.

In the UK the specialist education options for musically gifted school-age children are varied (and most are also open to overseas students). They include:

- centres of musical excellence
- choir or cathedral school
- junior department of a music college or conservatoire
- music scholarship to an independent school
- specialist music school

Centres of musical excellence In the UK there are a number of government-funded centres of excellence for musically talented children; in England they are officially known as Centres for Advanced Training. These bring together local and national teaching expertise (from music colleges and universities) with creative and performance expertise (from orchestras, opera companies and other professional musicians), and are often based around major venues such as concert halls and arts centres as well as using custom-built facilities.

The range of activities varies but all centres offer high-level music tuition to school-age students – usually integrated into a programme of other activities including performance and general music education. Tuition usually takes place outside of school hours – at weekends, after school and on holiday courses – giving talented children local access to a specialist music education while allowing them to continue with their current schooling. Means-tested grants towards the cost of fees are available through the government's Music and Dance Scheme.

▼▼▼ WEBWORDS centre + musical + excellence OR "Centre for Advanced Training" OR "Music and Dance Scheme"

Choir or cathedral school Around 35 schools in the UK are attached to cathedrals or churches and recruit young singers for their choirs. Most accept choristers between the ages of seven and nine, but some schools take children from as young as six. Some are for boys only, though the number of co-educational choir schools is increasing. Prospective choristers are selected after taking part in a voice trial, in which the choirmaster will be looking for a good musical ear, an enthusiasm for singing, and potential; they may also have to satisfy the school that they will be able to cope with the academic work alongside their musical commitments in the choir.

Not all the pupils will be choristers, and, unlike specialist music schools, not all the pupils will be musicians. But because music is such an important part of cathedral and church life, these schools often deliver an excellent music education, and not only in choral singing: academic music, bands, orchestras and other activities are likely to be strong, and there is usually access to excellent instrumental teaching.

Many choir schools have boarding facilities, although it is not always necessary for choristers to board. While the vast majority are independent schools and charge fees, scholarships are often granted to choristers – either from the school or through the government's Choir Schools' Scholarship Scheme. More information is available in the UK from the Choir Schools Association.

WEBWORDS "cathedral school" OR "choir school" + name of city or county ▼▼▼

Junior department of a music college or conservatoire Most music colleges and conservatoires have junior departments for younger pupils. These usually operate on Saturdays, but some open on weekday evenings as well. While very young children are taken at some, others accept only secondary-school pupils. Entry, by audition and interview, is usually very competitive. Fees vary, but scholarships and bursaries are sometimes available from the college, and financial support may be available for some students from their local education authority or through the government's Music and Dance Scheme.

Pupils normally study two musical instruments (many schools insist that one is a keyboard instrument); they will also receive coaching in ensemble and orchestral playing, and in singing. They study music theory and history, improvisation and composition; and other specialist classes may also be available.

Attending a junior department allows a young musician to remain in mainstream education while enjoying the benefits of a specialist music education. It takes care of most aspects of a child's music learning under one roof – often to a very high standard. While you shouldn't underestimate the amount of extra work and commitment involved (apart from Saturday attendance, there will be a rigorous practice schedule and possibly additional homework), children who attend a junior department usually find it immensely enjoyable and rewarding.

▼▼▼ WEBWORDS music + college OR conservatoire OR school
+ junior (department)

Music scholarship to an independent school Many fee-paying schools offer scholarships to talented young musicians. The application procedure, admissions policy, fees and conditions vary from school to school. Scholarships can pay for a large percentage of school fees (and in some instances there are extra funds for parents who may not be able to afford the remainder). Pupils who are awarded music scholarships are expected to play a major part in the school's musical life – singing in choirs, playing in orchestras, ensembles and bands, and encouraging other musicians – and music-making facilities are often excellent. The education is, however, more general than that offered by a specialist music school, and will not be geared specifically towards preparing children for a career in music.

▼▼▼ WEBWORDS music scholarship + independent school + mytown
OR mycounty OR mycountry

138

Specialist music school There are a small number of specialist music schools in the UK. Some take children from the age of eight, while others are open only to secondary-age pupils. Most have facilities for pupils to board. Fees vary, but means-tested grants (up to 100% of fees) are available from the government (through the Music and Dance Scheme), and some schools also award scholarships, so that exceptionally talented children are able to receive a specialist music education irrespective of their parent's ability to pay.

▼▼▼ WEBWORDS specialist music school + mycountry

At a specialist school, young musicians receive focused training from specialist staff in all areas of music. There will be a wide range of music-making and frequent opportunities to perform – music activities will take up a large proportion of the school's working week. These schools have strong links with professional musicians, music colleges, orchestras and other organizations, which allow pupils access to world-famous performers and teachers at masterclasses and concerts. Since specialist schools aim to provide pupils with the skills and attitudes they need to succeed as professional musicians, the curriculum may also include confidence-building, practical business skills and experience of life as a performer.

**Specialist schools aim to provide pupils with the skills and attitudes
they need to succeed as professional musicians.**

Most specialist schools have an emphasis on classical music, but all of them encourage pupils to learn a broad range of musical styles. A very small number concentrate on providing the skills required by pop, jazz and dance musicians (particularly music and recording technology in addition to performance). The UK also has a number of stage and theatre schools – independent organizations which teach the performing arts and prepare pupils for a career in show business and the entertainment industry. While the emphasis is on acting, dance and stagecraft, music is also studied. Stage school is a good option for pupils who display talent as pop performers, songwriters and dancers.

WEBWORDS stage school + mytown OR mycounty OR mycountry ▼▼▼

In the UK and many other countries, all full-time specialist schools are required by law to teach the standard school curriculum, so other aspects of a child's education are not neglected. If children return to mainstream education at any stage, they are therefore not disadvantaged in any way. Indeed, specialist schools often have high academic standards, and may be proud of their record of exam successes and university entrance in other subjects besides music – so after attending a specialist music school your child would still be able to go on to other things should he or she wish to.

Higher qualifications for talented younger pupils

Talented children who learn music from an early age, and who work consistently and enthusiastically, may reach a high standard quite early on. If they do well in music exams, it can be tempting to push them quickly through the higher grades. Yet these exams require a degree of musical maturity and understanding that, in many cases, will only emerge with time. Even those with fluent and advanced techniques may have trouble doing really well if their ability to express themselves musically is not similarly advanced. Nevertheless, it is by no means unusual for some pupils to pass Grade 8 at around the age of 14 or 15 (or even younger). What can they do next to maintain challenge and motivation and to prepare for the next level of music education?

139

You and your child might first study the examination mark sheet carefully (preferably with the teacher). If there are any weaknesses, these must be addressed in lessons. And consider how much music your child actually knows. If it is little beyond exam pieces, further study of a wider repertoire will be necessary. It may also be that your child would like to broaden his or her musical horizons by learning another instrument, having lessons in composition or improvisation, or exploring a new musical discipline (a jazz player might want to learn some classics, or vice versa). Participation at the higher levels in larger festivals and competitions will also help to boost performance skills.

There are further qualifications beyond Grade 8 if children are interested, and once the teacher feels that they are ready. Many of the exam boards now offer a performing exam at a higher level than Grade 8 which tests not only performance but also general musical knowledge and awareness. This may well be appropriate for capable young musicians who wish to take their studies further. For talented enthusiasts, or those who are considering music as a career, it may be possible while still at school to sit a diploma.

Diplomas demand a very high level of both technical proficiency and musicality. They often test knowledge of music theory and history, so it can be useful to be studying these at school (perhaps at A level or equivalent). There are many different diplomas, each with a different emphasis: some concentrate on performance, others on assessing teaching skills (a diploma in teaching is usually only available to students above the age of 18). If your child's regular teacher does not have much experience at this level, you might wish to arrange occasional lessons with a more specialist teacher, perhaps from a conservatoire or higher education college.

▼▼▼ WEBWORDS music + diploma + exam + mycountry
(or visit exam board websites)

Helping a talented child to deal with success

For the pre-adolescent gifted child, progress will usually be unhindered by psychological obstacles. Young children love mastering increasingly complex tasks and happily throw themselves into their music without inhibition. Adolescence, however, brings with it uncertainty, instability and a new set of impulses. It may not be coincidence that this is often also the point in a child's development when the musical gift first becomes really obvious – as children mature, so does their understanding of music and what they can do with it.

One major problem for adolescents is how to reconcile a desire for freedom from the family with the continued need for the family's love and support. Shrewd parents (and teachers) will prepare carefully for this time by allowing growing musicians the personal space they need. Talented children may have difficulty balancing their desire for independence with the need for a strict, extensive practice regime. Encourage practice but don't demand it. Most talented children will undertake the necessary work without much parental pressure, and their teachers will certainly expect it. Encourage also a broad range of music activity – solo playing, taking part in bands, ensembles, orchestras and choral singing. Help your child to see music as a passport to a wider world – a holiday course might enable him or her to meet students from different backgrounds and countries – but know when to step back and let your child take control.

Encourage practice but don't demand it.

For the exceptionally talented few – those who win high-profile competitions, for example – a career may begin much earlier than for most children. By the end of their school years they may already have performed extensively and achieved a certain renown. It is important to look at those who have achieved this kind of success (much has been written about them), and learn from both the high and the low points. Some have safely made the transition from child prodigy to mature adult and have become distinguished figures in the musical world; others have found their lives moving in confusing and unhappy directions.

Consider carefully therefore just how a career might develop. Slight changes of direction may be needed to avoid loss of interest or disillusionment: an instrumentalist may be advised to cultivate an interest in conducting or teaching, for example; or the learning of languages may be useful if an international career beckons. Sadly, the pressure of great success can bring its own emotional problems, particularly for young musicians. If problems do arise, counselling is an option; at the very least, young performers should be encouraged to maintain lines of discussion with teachers and other professional careers advisers.

Key points

- Very talented children need a lot of support.
- You and your child need to make decisions together, and they should be made for your child's sake, not yours.
- Your child's teacher is a vital source of support and advice, but you may need to seek help from other professionals too.
- Talented young musicians have a number of educational options – take your time to find out which is right for your child.
- Remember that success at a young age can bring its own problems.

Chapter 19

MUSIC IN FURTHER AND HIGHER EDUCATION

If your child goes from strength to strength as a developing musician during school years, he or she may well consider studying music at a more advanced level. This chapter will help you and your child to make decisions about taking music studies further at school, college or university. It looks first at further education, then at higher education, and considers some of the different qualifications and how they can prepare students for further study and careers. If your child already has a specific music career in mind, it might be useful to read this chapter along with Chapter 20.

Making choices

As they approach the current UK statutory school leaving age of 16, all young people need to decide whether to continue in education, and whether music will form part of that education. They should feel able to make their own decisions about their future, and the role of the parent now is to provide support in practical ways (encouraging children to obtain college prospectuses, taking them to open days etc.). Children should be allowed to trust their instincts and ability to find their own path.

The role of the parent now is to provide support in practical ways.

Further and higher education are not children's only means of progression into adulthood, however. For those who decide to leave school to get a job, music-making does not need to stop – young people can continue singing or learning an instrument, performing with others and deriving pleasure from it. As well as being enjoyable, this can provide a sense of continuity while other aspects of life are changing. And part-time educational options are available should young people wish to develop music further – indeed, many of the options offered as part of further education in music can be taken up part-time.

For those who decide to leave full-time education, music-making does not need to stop.

At 16, many developing musicians already have a sense of their abilities and potential. Those who have ambitions to play their instrument professionally should take advice from teachers and other musicians about how realistic this is, and which educational route to pursue. Those set on any career in music will benefit from some form of music qualification and should make music a central part of their further education.

At 16, many developing musicians already have a sense of their abilities and potential.

Others at this age may be less sure that they want a professional future in music but want to keep their options open – they, too, will benefit from studying music at an advanced level. This does not commit them to a career in music, since a music qualification can be an excellent basis for many other areas of study (especially if taken in conjunction with other subjects). Young musicians who have a deep love of music but have made up their minds to pursue non-musical careers may still want further education in music because they find it interesting and a good contrast with other subjects. The school should be able to advise on the qualifications that children will need for their chosen path.

As they begin to refine their educational choices, many young people feel that they want to abandon music-making altogether. The pressure of other studies may be too great or their social schedules may leave less time for music lessons, practice and playing. However, do encourage your child to continue with music at this stage, for it has many benefits. Firstly, music-making and its social aspects can be a welcome, healthy distraction from academic study. Secondly, in some countries (the UK included) higher grade music exams count as academic qualifications when calculating points for university entry. And finally, most educational establishments and employers prefer applicants to have plenty of interests beyond school; music-making will therefore count in young people's favour. Young musicians are likely to be self-motivated, and will have a considerable range of transferable skills: in addition to their abilities in music, they will have learned to be organized and will have developed good social skills. (Not all employers and places of education have the same attitude towards music qualifications, however, and some view them as less valuable than other more 'academic' subjects. If your child wishes to follow a specific educational or career path, it is worth finding out whether music will be regarded as a suitable qualification.)

Music-making and its social aspects can be a welcome, healthy distraction from academic study.

143

Higher grade music exams can count as academic qualifications when calculating points for university entry.

Further education

In the UK 'further education' means the period of education undertaken by students beyond the age of 16, during which a reduced range of subjects may be studied as preparation for higher education (which normally begins at 18) or a career.

For young musicians wishing to pursue their music studies there have traditionally been two main options: to study music as an academic subject (usually in tandem with instrumental lessons) to qualify for entry to university or music college; or to take vocational training in various aspects of music or music technology to prepare for a career in the music industry. Although the two types of qualification and approach remain, the distinctions between them are increasingly blurred: students usually have to display practical skills to gain academic qualifications, and vocational training tends to include a considerable amount of theoretical study.

To gain academic qualifications in music, such as AS (advanced subsidiary) and A (advanced) level in the UK, students follow a syllabus determined by various exam bodies (often associated with universities). These syllabuses each have their own content and it is the schools that decide which one to teach. In general, the exams require students to learn the history and theory of various styles of music. Performance is usually an option (students can choose to give a recital as part of the exam), as is composition (students are asked to produce scores and recordings of music they have written).

To gain practical or vocational qualifications, such as BTEC diplomas in the UK, students can take a wide range of courses including performance, music technology, studio production, songwriting, composition, marketing and administration. Some courses may also study the theoretical and historical aspects of music. Vocational training will not exclude your child from university or music college, and many young musicians now take this route to higher education. But since there are many different vocational qualifications, make sure – if your child is aiming at higher education – that you are properly informed about which course of further-education study is most appropriate.

There are many different vocational qualifications.
Make sure you are properly informed about
which is most appropriate.

At the time of writing, the UK government is launching a new set of diplomas for 14- to 19-year-olds that will combine classroom study with practical projects and work experience. These will be available at both schools and colleges. One of the diplomas on offer is a Creative and Media diploma, which will seek to develop a student's business skills alongside their creative and technical skills; this might be an alternative route for young people with an interest in music.

Further-education students have a range of choices about where to study. Many decide to remain at school, where they are likely to study for AS and A levels in a variety of subjects (some schools will now also offer the new diplomas). This is one of the most usual routes into higher education. An alternative is a sixth-form college – a larger establishment which takes students from a number of schools. Sixth-form colleges have certain advantages for musicians: they are of a greater size than school sixth-forms, so your child may be studying music with a larger group of students than at school; they can also offer good opportunities for music-making because all the students are of a similar age and level of commitment.

If your child is a skilled musician he or she may want to try for a place at one of the specialist music schools or for a music scholarship to an independent school. (For details of both, see Chapter 18.) Here there are likely to be large and flourishing sixth-form departments and excellent music facilities, with both practical and academic music taught to a high standard. Further Education (FE) colleges present different options: there is usually a wide range of vocational qualifications and many offer the chance to study AS and A levels too. Many specialist arts and music FE colleges are extremely well equipped for musicians, with recording studios, dedicated recital and concert halls, and practice rooms.

In the UK, full-time state education – whether in school, sixth-form college or FE college – is free for 16- to 19-year-olds. Independent schools will charge fees, and there may be charges for courses at other privately run organizations. Grants and subsidies may be available from the government (to help with the cost of transport, books or other materials), the local education authority or charitable institutions.

WEBWORDS "further education" + grant ▼▼▼
(also see local education authority website)

Higher education

Towards the end of further-education studies, students are faced with another set of decisions about what to do. If they decide to continue into higher education, prospective music students should get advice from their school or college, and from instrumental teachers. Most places of higher education offer open days, and pupils should attend one or two to get a feel not just for their proposed course of study but for the environment in which they may be spending the next three or four years. In addition to studying prospectuses, they should try to talk to present or former students of their favoured institutions. Essentially, young musicians have the following options:

- music college or conservatoire
- university
- other places of higher education

145

Music college or conservatoire For the aspiring performer, music college may be the right choice. These institutions have a large number of professional musicians on the staff, many of them performers themselves. There will also be visits from internationally famous musicians who give lectures and masterclasses. The emphasis will be on practical music-making in its many forms, and on preparing the student for life as a professional musician. (Many courses take the latter point quite seriously and offer advice on self-promotion, dealing with prospective employers and numerous other vocational issues.) Music colleges also offer classes in music history and theory, and often in other subjects that musicians are likely to need, such as modern languages. Most conservatoires focus on training students from a classical background who have ambitions to work in this area, although many of them also have excellent facilities for jazz and pop musicians and some offer courses in folk and traditional music.

At music college, the emphasis will be on practical music-making in its many forms, and on preparing the student for life as a professional musician.

To qualify for music college, students will need A level music or an equivalent vocational qualification. Students are also likely to require other further-education qualifications such as additional A levels or a higher-level vocational certificate. But the prime requirement will be for students to display a high level of musical skill – or at least a lot of potential – both on their chosen instrument (or voice) and in general musicianship. This will be tested by audition, and some colleges ask students to sit a written examination. Additionally, some specify that students must have reached a minimum practical level on their instrument of choice – 'fluency to Grade 8 standard' if not the exam result itself.

For many students the choice of teachers at a particular college may have a significant bearing on their decision regarding where to apply. It can be useful to arrange a consultation lesson with a preferred teacher before making an application, as your child may learn much that may affect a final decision over the application. However, as many colleges will not guarantee your first-choice teacher, the position here needs to be investigated in advance. Other factors to consider include the range of courses available, the music facilities, the opinions of past students, and practical matters like accommodation.

University Traditionally, university was seen as being for those with a more academic interest in music, while music colleges were felt to be for those who wish predominantly to study performance. The dividing line is now much less distinct. Increasingly, universities are offering a range of practical courses like music technology, electronic music and studio production, while music colleges, sometimes in conjunction with nearby universities, offer significant academic components. Yet students with a real desire to learn the academic side of music still usually choose university.

All universities prepare their own courses, and the content and relative proportion of different subjects within a course can be quite diverse. When applying for a university place, therefore, students need to send off for prospectuses and study them carefully. Courses at universities at the more traditional end of the spectrum usually include subjects such as music history, musicology and analysis (the theoretical study of how music is written and constructed), ethnomusicology (the study of music from different cultures), musical aesthetics (the philosophy of music as an art form), and composition. Generally, the practical content of the courses is considerably less than at a music college (though all students will be expected to sing or play an instrument to a reasonable standard, and to have a high level of general musicianship). Entrance requirements for a music course at university will normally include a number of A levels, one of which will be music. Vocational and practical qualifications are often acceptable as well.

Generally, the practical content of university music courses is less than at a music college.

Musicians with an interest in performing may well benefit from university too. It is important to look closely at the actual weighting of practical music within the syllabus – on some courses it is a relatively small part, but a number of universities now give students the opportunity to tailor the shape of their own study. Enterprising players will be able to form ensembles and set up concerts. Some university departments provide practical lessons (instrumental and vocal) for students. A number organize and pay for students to have lessons with distinguished teachers outside the university; others make no provision, and leave it to individuals to find teachers. Students will need to establish who will pay for instrumental lessons and whether or not there is the possibility of subsidy (especially if travel is involved). At university, performing musicians often have a surprising range of opportunities, as there may be less competition than at music college.

Some pupils who attach even weighting to their practical and their academic studies, and may be undecided as to which direction to take, could be offered places at both music college and university. Under these circumstances they may like to take up the university course first and then go on to music college as a postgraduate, thereby getting the best of both worlds. It should, nevertheless, be taken into account that the standard required for entry to music college as a postgraduate is usually very high, and that these courses are both sought after and expensive.

Music college followed by university is a less desirable strategy for those wishing to pursue a performing career, as the important impetus and contacts

147

made may be lost. However, for those who want to work in teaching or music administration, for example, this may be both effective and useful. A few music colleges offer combined courses with local universities. These courses are normally very challenging and extremely hard work. In addition, they vary enormously in their provision for lessons and performing opportunities, and should therefore be examined very carefully.

Other places of higher education Some specialist arts and performance colleges offer degrees and diplomas in music, and may in fact provide a wider range of practical tuition for those students whose interests and skills are not normally catered for by music college or university. At these institutions, students can take courses in such subjects as performance, media technology, radio and television, librarianship, music publishing, instrument making, band and event management, and journalism. Entrance requirements differ according to the course and the institution in question. Many of these courses are ideal for students who have already decided on a career path (for more on this, see Chapter 20). For those who remain unsure what their career will be, it is advisable to obtain a broad-based music education first before specializing later.

Key points

- There are many options for students who wish to continue music into further and higher education.

- Young people who decide not to study music at a higher level will still benefit from the social and creative aspects of continuing to make music.

- The choice of educational pathway is for your child to make, not you – but your support is still valuable.

- If your child has a particular career in mind, make sure that he or she makes educational choices that will lead to the necessary qualifications.

Chapter 20

MUSIC AS A CAREER

There are many ways in which an interest in music can become the basis of a fulfilling (and financially rewarding) working life. If parents are informed about the options, they can help their children to make some of the decisions or at least help them to follow a particular route.

This chapter looks at some of the ways in which people make a living with music. It also considers some of the qualifications, skills and experience that may be needed in each area.

Routes to a career in music

Some young people appear to know very early on that they wish to work professionally in some music-related area; others realize this more gradually. For some, opportunities present themselves as a result of music education: as both ability and knowledge develop, options for the future begin to emerge. A young musician who frequently wins high-level competitions may feel that he or she has the potential to become a professional performer (and the opinions of others may reinforce this impression) – or a teenager with an outstanding ability as a songwriter may hope for a composing career. Others may find that the path is less obvious – and maybe less glamorous – but they are still motivated by a real interest in music and are determined to succeed. It might take time for your child's ultimate direction to emerge, but it is far better to consider fully the range of possibilities than to jump in hurriedly and risk making demoralizing mistakes.

> **It might take time for your child's ultimate direction as a musician to emerge.**

If undertaking further or higher education in music, your child may well be considering the option of pursuing a career with music. While music education is vital to later success as a professional, the route in to a career can be complex and no two people have the same experience. Only the tiniest minority will find themselves catapulted to superstar status after college or university. For the majority, the beginning of their career will be slower and less spectacular, though it may be no less rewarding and exciting. Some professional musicians take many years to establish a reputation, often working at a number of different activities in different contexts, moving between them according to circumstances. (For many jobs, experience and transferable skills gained in this way can be an advantage.) For example, many performers also teach; some teachers become trainers of other teachers, examiners for the exam boards, or writers about music (in music education, for example). Even within one discipline there may be many different opportunities: most performers and teachers are likely to work with a range of groups and in many settings. But regardless of the job in question, the key qualities that musicians will need in employment are reliability and flexibility.

The route in to a music career can be complex and no two people have the same experience.

Building a sustainable career in music takes time, and requires talent, commitment and luck. Young people should be encouraged to take as many musical opportunities as possible – performing, listening to others perform, organizing concerts, or attending courses and schemes where they will meet other musicians. Such courses not only bolster confidence and increase knowledge but also offer the chance to build up a network of contacts, which can be all-important for securing later work. These contacts often support musicians over many years, since people are usually much happier employing those whom they know personally or have heard a lot about.

▼▼▼ WEBWORDS music + career + advice

Jobs in music tend to be sought after and young people need to be prepared to compete to get them. But because music career structures are often quite informal, it is not unusual for one job to lead to another, or for a short period of clerical work in, say, a record company office to grow into a more permanent post with better prospects and training. It is particularly true of music that, in many cases, young people should also be encouraged to try several different career paths – the more varied their experience, the more valued they are likely to be. If a job candidate has some experience of performing, teaching, music technology and organizing events, his or her skills may be more desirable than someone who has concentrated on just one of these areas. Other useful attributes include a talent for self-promotion and, particularly in the early stages, a degree of self-sacrifice (taking an unpaid work-experience job, for instance) – being seen to be willing and able will always be a good approach.

The more varied a young person's experience, the more valued they are likely to be.

Career options

Some careers are more obvious than others and so more immediately appealing to young people. For example, young performers may be enthralled by the idea of giving concerts, touring the world and playing or singing, because they see constant media evidence of this. They may be less aware that for every television appearance of a star performer, hundreds of other people are professionally involved – among them concert promoters, artists' agents, sound and recording technicians, instrument manufacturers and publishers. For this reason it will be useful to make your child aware of the full range of options that is available to them.

There is a huge range of music-related careers, as the following list indicates. Each area of occupation describes what the work involves, and suggests the kind of qualifications, skills and experience that might be needed.

A&R see *Artists and repertoire*

Accompanist see *Performing: Accompanist*

Artist management Artist management agencies organize the day-to-day work of performing musicians. They deal with many of the practicalities of arranging concerts, negotiate fees for performances and recordings, ensure that performers are in the right place at the right time, and make travel and accommodation arrangements. Most solo performers, and many other free-lance instrumentalists, employ an artist management company to promote and run their careers. Work in artist management requires a wide knowledge of music, musicians and performance opportunities; excellent organizational skills; and also a talent for diplomacy and negotiation. Experience of organizing amateur concerts or similar events may be useful. Foreign languages and some knowledge of the law can also be advantageous.

Artists and repertoire (A&R) Record companies – whatever the genre of music – are always in need of new performers and composers or songwriters. To find these individuals, they employ A&R executives who seek out talent by going to concerts featuring new artists, watching performance videos and listening to audition recordings. Some A&R executives are also responsible for managing the careers of established musicians, forming the link between the performer and the record company. Work in A&R requires a wide and detailed knowledge of music in the relevant style, and a highly developed sense of trends and markets. A music degree, experience of working in a recording studio or in music retail, and some knowledge of business and marketing are all desirable.

Arts and music administration A wide range of organizations employ arts administrators: these include festivals, venues, orchestras, opera and ballet companies, community-based groups, educational charities, local authorities and funding bodies. Tasks might range from programming, booking performers and organizing events to marketing, fund-raising and front-of-house management. Employees of funding bodies, such as the Arts Councils in the UK, may spend time reviewing the work of a musician or artist, for example, to assess whether it should qualify for receipt of funding. Some arts administrators, particularly those in smaller organizations, might be required to work in all areas of the arts and may need to fulfil a variety of different roles. The job requires a broad knowledge of the arts, organizational ability, and good business and communication skills. Experience of organizing amateur events – at university or college, perhaps – is useful. Several colleges and universities in the UK offer postgraduate degrees and diplomas in arts administration; others run shorter training courses. Many festivals employ temporary staff and a number of arts organizations offer voluntary placements; these are often excellent ways to gain experience and make contacts.

Broadcasting There are a number of opportunities for music-related work in radio and television, working either for national or regional broadcasters or for the many independent production companies commissioned by radio and television stations to make programmes. These organizations need journalists (see *Journalism*, below) to find stories, develop programme ideas, and write and edit scripts. Presenters are needed to deliver the programmes. If the broadcasts are music-related, the presenters will require a high level of musical knowledge in addition to journalism skills.

On the technical side, studio engineers are responsible for setting up and recording programmes (see also *Recording engineer*, below); many colleges offer courses in radio and television engineering. Producers are responsible for coordinating all the different elements – technical, artistic and financial – that create a programme. To work as a producer requires both technical knowledge and journalistic experience; music producers need knowledge of (and interest in) a wide range of music, and some experience of performing can help. A university music degree, followed by broadcast training, is probably the best route here, though any amateur journalism or broadcasting experience will help too.

Community music Many musicians work in places and with people who do not otherwise have access to music-making. Community music workers can be found in many different types of setting (for instance hospitals, prisons, factories and housing estates) where they involve members of the community in music-making projects. In some cases these have a specific educational aim, or a therapeutic purpose (see also *Music therapy*, below), but often music-making is encouraged in these settings simply because it is enjoyable and builds people's confidence and sense of togetherness. Most community musicians are employed (usually on a freelance basis) by arts or education organizations, or by small specialist groups; some opera companies and orchestras also employ community music workers. Community musicians need to be versatile, adaptable and able to inspire people who may never have experienced any music-making. Teaching, performing, composing and administration skills will all be useful. Some colleges and universities provide courses in community music.

Composing There is always a demand for new music. Composers come from all kinds of backgrounds, and their training and experience varies. Many university and music college courses offer composition as an option, and it is often studied formally at postgraduate level. Composers – in whatever style they write – need patience and determination, and must be prepared to seek out their own opportunities by promoting themselves (using the Internet is a good way to do this) and sending samples of their work, recorded or in print, to publishers and record companies. (Any samples – on paper or recorded – need to be professionally presented.) Composers are also now likely to need considerable skills in music technology. A number of options for composers are listed below:

Concert music Few composers of contemporary classical music make a living from writing concert music alone – most also teach, perform, conduct, or run their own ensembles. Some compose, arrange and edit for film and media (see below) as well as for the concert hall. It can take many years to develop a career as a concert composer. Young writers can find it difficult to get their work performed, and need to rely on income from competitions, grants and awards. Once well-known, however, composers can earn money from commissions (writing to order for a particular event, ensemble or soloist) and from royalties (income from performances, broadcasts, and sales of recordings and sheet music).

153

Educational music Many composers write specifically for children and young people who are learning to play, and there is a large market for educational music of this sort. This work is usually commissioned by music publishers (see *Publishing*, below). Composers writing educational music usually need experience of instrumental teaching or related educational matters so that they are aware of young musicians' interests and capabilities.

Film Composing music for films can be very well paid, but it is extremely specialized. As well as being able to write music to order, film composers need highly developed technical skills, the ability to work quickly under pressure, and good powers of negotiation and diplomacy. Many film composers are experienced composers for radio and television (see *Media*, below); others have a background in recording or sound engineering.

Established film composers often have teams of assistants who help with scoring, arranging and recording – obtaining such a role is often a good pathway into the industry. A wide knowledge of film, and of the way in which music is used in film, is useful. Many universities and colleges offer an option in film music.

Media Industries such as broadcasting (radio and television), advertising, and new digital media (computer games and phone ringtones) constantly demand new music. Most large music publishing companies have specialist departments which are set up to supply 'media music' to a range of clients. They employ composers (almost always on a freelance basis) in a variety of ways – to provide music for individual projects or to write 'library music' (music which is pre-composed and recorded, then promoted and sold 'off-the-shelf' to radio and television stations or advertising companies).

To work in media music, a composer needs to be quick and efficient, capable of writing in a variety of styles, and able to interpret the client's requirements. Since media departments always need new and different music, they sometimes accept 'showreels' (recordings of sample material) from composers looking for work. Any recordings submitted in this way need to be of the highest possible quality. Several music colleges now offer excellent courses in writing and recording for media.

Songwriting Pop, rock and jazz songwriters can make a living in two different ways – either performing and recording their own songs (see *Performing*, below) or writing for other performers. Many well-known songwriters began their careers as performers but turned to writing for other artists. The royalty income from publishing and recording, particularly of pop music, can be very considerable.

New songwriters need to get their music heard by record companies and publishers – either by advertising their performances or by sending samples of their work (preferably recorded) to A&R departments, or even to performers themselves. Once again, the Internet is an excellent tool for this. Most songwriters – in addition to being creative – will need technical skills (computer or recording studio) and an ability to market their work and seek out opportunities for it. A number of university and college courses – particularly those with an emphasis on pop music – offer modules in songwriting.

Theatre There are many different ways in which composers can work in the theatre, from composing incidental music for plays and other productions to writing full-scale works like musicals. Amateur experience of theatre music is often a useful route in – as is general experience of composing and an ability to write music in a wide variety of styles. Most composers for the theatre will be expected to be able to play a variety of instruments, sing, direct other musicians, and score and arrange music for all sorts of performers, instruments and skill levels. Some music colleges (particularly those with drama departments) offer courses which focus on creating music for productions.

Conducting Most conductors train first as instrumentalists or singers, at music college or university. They usually gain experience from working with amateur and semi-professional orchestras and choirs, building a reputation over time. There are also a number of postgraduate courses in conducting. Conductors need wide musical understanding and skills, particularly sharp hearing and attention to detail, a broad and deep knowledge of repertoire, and good communication, management and leadership skills. As well as directing orchestras, bands, large ensembles and choirs, conductors can find work as musical directors in the theatre (see *Performing: Theatre*, below), in film music and in community music projects (see *Community music*, above).

DJing DJs work in two main areas: clubs (where they play and mix dance music, with little or no speaking involved) and radio (where they are required as much for their speaking skills as their playing of recorded music). Some DJs do both radio and club work, though opportunities for radio work are more limited; the majority of DJs are employed in clubs, bars, and holiday and entertainment venues. Many run their own businesses, playing at special events and parties. Any DJ must be familiar with a huge variety of music, and know the market well. Good business, marketing and organizational skills are essential, and an ability with technology even more so. Good DJs can find live work through entertainment agencies. Radio DJs often start their careers with a technical position at a radio station – engineering or producing shows (see also *Broadcasting*, above). Some colleges offer courses in DJing, club management and broadcasting techniques.

Events management Some venues have staff who plan future events and programmes. There are also independent companies who set up, finance and promote concerts and other music events, book artists, and organize publicity and advertising. Although elements of this work can be similar to arts administration (see above), events management companies tend to operate within the private sector and may be more concerned with the organization of an individual event than the development of larger arts programmes and festivals. Marketing, legal and business skills, together with practical experience of organizing shows and performances, are vital. Knowledge of music (and particularly music technology) may also be useful.

Film music see *Composing: Film*

Information technology (IT) Most musicians use IT (computers and software) as a toolkit to help them in their specific area of work. Recording engineers will use recording software; composers and engravers (those who

155

prepare printed music for publication) are likely to use notation software (see *Publishing* and *Music engraving*); and teachers may use all kinds of technology to help motivate their pupils. There are also jobs for those who create the software in the first place: music software developers operate all over the world. To work in music-related IT, it's necessary to have experience of both music and music software. Some universities offer courses in music-related software engineering or computer science – either as part of a computer science degree in collaboration with a music department, or as an option within a music degree.

Instrument making Opportunities in instrument manufacture range from the creation of hand-made, custom-built items to the design and construction of mass-produced equipment. Skilled technicians are also required for instrument maintenance and repair; some will be employed by instrument retailers to work in their repair workshops, though others, particularly piano tuners, might be self-employed. For craft-based work, experience and qualifications in woodwork and metalwork are useful. Specialist instrument makers, such as those who build violins and guitars by hand, often develop their skills over many years and slowly acquire a list of clients: this requires most importantly an ability to create the instruments but also some skills in marketing and self-promotion. Many colleges now offer courses in instrument manufacture and maintenance. To work in research and development of electronic instruments and equipment, knowledge of electronics and acoustics is needed. Some university science departments offer courses in related areas, sometimes in conjunction with music departments.

IT see *Information technology*

Journalism Most newspaper writers find their jobs after a general training in journalism, and will write about a range of subjects. Music specialists in these organizations are rare, though some do employ music critics (writers who review concerts and recordings), usually on a freelance basis. Specialists may be more suited to a job on a dedicated music journal or magazine, though once again most of the work for writers tends to be freelance (and often irregular). Skills in journalism are of course vital, and these can be acquired through experience and also from postgraduate journalism courses at colleges and universities. A music journalist also needs a wide knowledge and deep understanding of music – and the ability to communicate it to the reader. In radio and television journalism, music specialists are very rare; an arts correspondent will be expected to cover music alongside a wide variety of other subjects (see also *Broadcasting*, above).

Librarianship Music librarians work in a number of different contexts – and not just in libraries and museums. Many of the larger orchestras and opera companies need librarians to organize, catalogue and control use of their performance materials (scores and parts); colleges and universities need music specialists to run their collections; and a number of broadcasters employ librarians to manage their recordings and archives. Some of the larger music publishers run 'hire libraries', which supply orchestral parts to professional and amateur orchestras for rehearsal and performance. Music librarians need to be able to read music and should have a broad knowledge of music history (a music degree may be advisable for this). A librarianship qualification (often studied at postgraduate level) is desirable and will be essential for certain posts.

Media In the music industry, 'media' often refers to the creation of music for radio and television (see *Composing: Media*). For music opportunities in radio and television, see *Broadcasting* and *Journalism.*

Music engraving / music setting Music engravers create the printed music found in scores and books. This used to be done by hand; nowadays it is chiefly done by computer, but still conforms to old-established and complex rules of design and layout. Music engraving is required by music publishers and by any organization or individual needing materials from which musicians can play. Most (though not all) music engravers are qualified musicians, but an eye for detail, a feel for graphic design, and an ability to work accurately and quickly are all essential. Experienced engravers will find their skills much in demand.

157

Music therapy Music therapists work in schools, hospitals, hospices, clinics, and community settings. They use music as a means of communicating with the client for a variety of purposes: to build confidence and self-esteem, to resolve emotional and behavioural problems, to soothe physical pain, and to encourage self-expression. Music is here a means of therapy rather than a subject that is taught. In the UK music therapists must be trained and formally qualified before they can register with the Health Professions Council as a practising music therapist. A number of colleges and universities offer postgraduate courses in music therapy; prospective students usually have a degree or diploma in music, and must be able to demonstrate experience of (or motivation to) work in this field and a high level of musicianship. (There is more about music therapy in Chapter 17.)

Performance is the public face of music.

Performing Performance is the public face of music: it is the aim and ambition of many musicians, and it is also what the word 'musician' suggests to most people. For performing musicians there is a huge range of opportunities. Life as a performer, however, can be tough and it is always competitive – to be in demand, professional singers and players have to maintain a very high standard. A lot of daily practice is needed to keep technical skills at their peak. In addition, there is often a great deal of travel involved (for instance when touring with a band, orchestra or theatre company), and performers may find that they have only a short time to learn new music and adapt to new surroundings. But many performers find that the challenges make their work extremely rewarding.

Most performers make a living in a range of different ways, and are likely to work on a freelance basis, gradually developing their career and, with it, a reputation. For most of the areas of performance listed below, performers will require training (see Chapter 19) and wide experience of music-making. If a young performer has a particular area of interest and expertise, it will be necessary to investigate all the opportunities that relate to it specifically, and these vary widely. A skilled performer of traditional or ethnic music, for example, will require specialist teaching and may need to find particular community-based outlets for performing and recording. Or a young brass, woodwind or percussion player may consider a career with a military band (the armed forces provide a number of opportunities for musicians).

Accompanist/repetiteur Many pianists find work accompanying singers and instrumentalists in lessons, exams, recitals and rehearsals. Repetiteurs are pianists employed by opera and ballet companies (and classes) to play for rehearsals. This work requires highly developed musicianship skills: sight-reading, the ability to play at the piano from an orchestral score, and transposition. Some music colleges offer courses for accompanists and repetiteurs.

Backing musician see *Session musician*

Church or cathedral musician Some of the larger churches and cathedrals employ musicians on a regular basis as music directors, organists and singers. However, these are not always full-time and most church musicians supplement their income by other means – usually concert performances and teaching. The post of church music director normally involves training and conducting a choir, so experience of singing and vocal coaching will be essential, as will knowledge of the church music repertoire and tradition.

Ensemble performance Small groups of musicians – for example string quartets, wind quintets, brass quintets or small jazz bands – are much in demand both at public venues and private events. Some performers form their own groups, practising and performing together, developing a repertoire and an individual style, and often building a reputation over time. Playing in these small groups requires a particular set of skills: a very high technical and musical standard (players are especially exposed in small groups in intimate venues or on recordings), and an ability to work extremely closely with other musicians. Most music colleges insist that students study chamber music and work in small ensembles as part of their coursework.

Jazz Jazz requires a special set of musical and technical skills which are largely outside the classical tradition – the ability to improvise (make up music on the spot) and to be instantly and creatively responsive to another player or players in a variety of musical contexts. These skills are often developed over many years from studying with jazz teachers and playing in jazz groups. Performers can find opportunities with their own bands, as soloists with various ensembles and as session musicians.

Orchestral playing A good proportion of orchestral players work for one of the permanent touring symphony orchestras (or larger opera companies). For some instrumentalists – string players especially – it is possible to have a formal career structure within an orchestra, being promoted to a more prominent position as experience grows: in this way performers might work for the same orchestra for many years. Others prefer to vary their career, working freelance in a variety of ways – deputizing in permanent orchestras (filling in for absent or unavailable musicians, or supplementing when extra musicians are needed) or playing in a variety of orchestras put together for recording sessions (see *Session musician*, below) or one-off concerts. Orchestral players need excellent technical and musical skills, and good sight-reading is important, as players often need to learn new pieces very quickly. Playing in youth orchestras is the best way to start building the essential foundations, and music colleges offer specialist teaching in many different aspects of orchestral playing – they are an excellent place to gain further orchestral experience and many have training links with major orchestras.

159

Pop and rock The traditional routes to fame for pop musicians rely on talent, persistence and luck. It is possible for musicians to form a band, write songs, perform in public, build up a following, and be signed by a record company – but it is an extremely competitive world and there are thousands of people chasing a similar dream. (Other more 'instant' approaches such as high-profile talent competitions are increasingly common, but rarely offer long-term career solutions.)

> **The traditional routes to fame for pop musicians rely on talent, persistence and luck.**

From the outside, life as a pop star can seem very glamorous, but the realities – particularly in the early years of a musician's career – are hard work, constant touring, being under pressure to write and record new material, and coping with the constant media attention. There is an additional difficulty in that pop careers are short-lived for all but a very small minority. In an industry that thrives on novelty, stardom can fade very quickly and replacements are always available.

To have a hope of signing a record contract, any new band or performer will need to be able to demonstrate originality, considerable experience of live performance, and drive and commitment. Performers need to be excellent at self-promotion to achieve success: an Internet presence is increasingly important. A well-produced demo – an audio (or, better still, video) recording featuring samples of the band's work – will be vital, and this should be sent to the A&R department of record companies, radio and television stations, live venues, and music journalists. Many colleges offer courses in pop, rock, jazz and traditional music, teaching a range of skills from composing, songwriting and recording techniques to marketing, promotion and business management.

Session musician Record companies, film companies, broadcasters, independent production companies and advertising agencies are just some of the organizations that frequently require newly recorded music. It is not usually economical for them to employ musicians full-time, so they organize recording sessions as necessary. Sessions can range from a few pop vocalists singing a radio jingle to a full-scale orchestra recording a film soundtrack.

Session musicians need to be excellent sight-readers (in jazz and pop they may be required to perform from chord charts and informal notation). They also need to be adaptable, and able to work in a variety of styles and to perform well under pressure, because studio time is often limited. Although session work can be quite well-paid and varied, it is sporadic and therefore not a source of regular income at first. However, session musicians with a reputation for reliability and adaptability are always in demand. There are agencies that specialize in booking musicians for sessions, and there are also a number of orchestras, choirs and other groups that specialize in session work.

Singing Singers can take rather longer than other musicians to find a career path, as the voice needs a long time to develop. Singers are encouraged not to start training too early, so may wait until their early 20s to explore the possibility of a professional career. Most classical singers perform in a variety of contexts – in opera, in concerts (as a soloist or with a professional choir), or in recitals with an accompanist. They may also find work with cathedral and church choirs (many singers begin their careers in this way before moving on to become soloists). Singers in all styles are sometimes required for broadcast and session work (see *Session musician*, above).

Singers can take rather longer than other musicians to find a career path, as the voice needs a long time to develop.

Solo performance Very few performers make a living from solo performance alone. The pressures are enormous because the competition is so fierce. Soloists often gain recognition as a result of winning high-profile competitions and giving regular performances (often touring for many months of the year). However, it can take a number of years – and exceptional talent and great determination – to establish a career as a world-class soloist. Along the way, most performers will undertake some ensemble work, and possibly a little orchestral playing too; they may also teach and give masterclasses. Successful soloists make money from both public performances and recordings – contracts with the major record companies are hard to obtain but can be financially very worthwhile. Most soloists will have an agent to manage their workload and negotiate fees and contracts.

Theatre Theatres often require live music, with musicals and other shows needing large pit orchestras, and many plays needing small bands to play incidental music. Most theatres employ an agency to recruit musicians for a particular production. Theatre musicians need to be prepared to play the same show every night, often for weeks or months – but also need to be adaptable enough to respond to changes that occur during individual performances. A musical director will be responsible for specifying the show's requirements, arranging and organizing the music, and rehearsing and training the performers and orchestra. Certain music colleges – particularly those with drama departments – offer courses in theatre-music direction. Experience of amateur and student productions is invaluable.

Producer see *Broadcasting* and *Record industry*

Publishing Music publishers occupy a central position in the music supply chain. They are responsible for finding and contracting composers and songwriters, and promoting their work to the various people who will want to use it. The A&R department (see *Artists and repertoire*, above) will seek out new writers. Other departments will be dedicated to promotion (finding performance, broadcast, licensing and recording opportunities for the company's copyrights); copyright management (protecting the company's copyrights from infringement and maximizing their value – see *Rights management*, below); and royalty collection and distribution (collecting usage fees from clients and distributing it to composers). There might also be a media department (see *Composing: Media*, above) dedicated to the creation and promotion of music to the broadcast and advertising industries.

> **Music publishers occupy a central position in the music supply chain.**

Many classical music publishers have departments that create performance materials for new works – these require skilled editors (often freelance) and copyists (people who create music parts for professional use). In addition, there may be a hire library, which supplies orchestral parts (for a fee) to professional and amateur orchestras for rehearsal and performance.

Some publishers also have print music departments that create publications for sale – mostly to the educational or leisure markets. Products might include anything from repertoire volumes, tutor books, educational CDs and other multimedia resources to vocal scores, chamber music and study scores. These departments employ a range of freelance staff including writers, editors, composers, arrangers, designers, proofreaders, recording engineers and music engravers (see *Music engraving*, above).

The many different jobs in music publishing need different skills, qualifications and experience – but most will require a music degree. Depending on the specific area of the business, legal skills, business and marketing experience, a teaching qualification, and knowledge of performance or recording may be useful.

Record industry Most record companies employ staff to do very particular jobs. These include: producers (executives responsible for coordinating recordings and devising new projects); A&R (see *Artists and repertoire*, above); sales, marketing and promotional staff; and those responsible for administering copyrights, contracts and royalties (see *Rights management*, below). (Few record companies have their own recording facilities; the actual making of recordings in studios is usually done independently by specially commissioned engineers – see *Recording engineer*, below.) Most record industry staff have either a degree or a diploma in a music-related subject, though general experience in the arts, marketing or law can be equally useful in certain departments.

Recording engineer/sound engineer Specialists in sound recording and projection are required in recording studios, theatres, concert halls, and other indoor and outdoor venues, as well as by broadcasters. Some recording engineers are employed full-time by studios; others are engaged on a freelance basis by producers in record companies or broadcasting organizations. Recording engineers need to be highly skilled in all types of recording technology: colleges and universities offer a variety of training courses, some of them linked to professional studios and recording organizations. Practical experience of home recording and music technology, together with keen ears and musical knowledge, will be very useful.

Sound engineers may not work in recording studios, but provide amplification for performance venues. Though many have a background in music, knowledge of acoustics and music technology is just as important. Again, courses in music technology, acoustics and sound engineering are offered by many universities and music colleges.

Retail Music shops sell musical instruments (acoustic and electronic), sheet music and books about music, recording equipment, and accessories. A good knowledge of the subject and the market is required. The ability to demonstrate by performing on instruments is an advantage, and teaching experience can also be useful. Some specialist shops may require assistants to have a particular skill. For example, many guitar dealers employ a technician to make minor repairs and ensure that instruments leave the shop in optimum condition. Dealers in music technology may require assistants to be knowledgeable about computer software and hardware.

Rights management Record, media and publishing companies own and manage copyrights on behalf of their composers and performers. The copyright of any newly published composition or recording is protected so that the creator and publisher can earn money from it and control its use. Publishers and recording companies have departments that negotiate with other organizations who want to publish, perform, record or broadcast their copyrights. These will also ensure that copyrights are not being infringed (used illegally without payment). Music copyright executives usually have a wide knowledge of music, and may also have legal or business qualifications. Some legal firms have media departments that employ specialists in copyright law. (See also *Publishing* and *Artists and repertoire.*)

Songwriting see *Composing*

Teaching Music teachers need excellent communication skills and the ability to inspire and motivate; they must be creative, adaptable and patient. Instrumental teachers need a good grasp of the instrument and the ability to pass this on to others. Flexibility and the ability to tailor their teaching to the needs of the pupil are also essential. (There is more about this in Chapter 6.)

163

Teachers can find work in many different settings (and may have to specify a preference when beginning training). Some teachers, particularly those outside a school setting, combine more than one type of teaching – they may work peripatetically, visiting schools, and also have a number of private pupils.

> An ability to communicate well with young children
> may be the most important skill of all.

Early years Musicians can work in a number of different contexts with pre-school and nursery children. Some are employed by local education authorities and music services to work within nursery schools and other childcare settings – for this, some formal teaching or childcare qualification (though not necessarily music-related) will be necessary. Others develop a private teaching practice delivering music activities for young children – sometimes in conjunction with a commercial organization, sometimes on an individual basis. For this, it is important to have teaching or childcare experience and some knowledge of music (and music education issues for the very young). Formal qualifications are not always obligatory, however, and an ability to communicate well with young children may be the most important skill of all.

Peripatetic/school instrumental teaching Many instrumental teachers in the UK are employed by music services (organizations contracted by local education authorities to provide music tuition in state schools and at music centres). This often involves travelling from school to school and teaching in a variety of settings – sometimes working with groups of children, sometimes with individuals, sometimes in the classroom. Independent schools often have large music departments and will employ specialists on most instruments. Most music services require teachers to have a teaching qualification; this may not be necessary in the independent sector although it is still desirable.

Private instrumental teaching The general attributes of an instrumental teacher need here to be supplemented by good business skills, in order to run an efficient teaching practice. While a teaching qualification is not obligatory for private teachers, it is desirable and may be required by potential clients. A teaching diploma or degree from a music college will often include elements of the philosophy of teaching, case studies and theory, and will require a broad knowledge of the instrument and its repertoire. Some professional organizations, including ABRSM, offer instrumental teaching qualifications.

School music teaching In the UK there are few music specialists in primary schools: most primary teachers are generalists who teach all subjects. However, many schools have one or two teachers with special responsibility for music – these people have often studied music, but need not have a formal qualification. At middle and senior school level, children learn music (compulsory up to the age of 14 in the UK) from specialist teachers who usually have a degree in music and a formal teaching qualification (or a degree in teaching with a music specialism).

School music teachers need enormous stamina, good organizational skills, and the ability to deliver a curriculum; they also need to communicate well with children at all levels of ability. Classroom music teachers are usually also expected to take responsibility for general musical life within school, running choirs, orchestras, bands, concerts and other productions. This can be rewarding, but it can also mean long hours and considerable extra work.

Teaching in further and higher education The older the pupils, the more specialized teaching may become. In further education, music teachers may have a music degree and a teaching qualification –

particularly those teaching GCSE, AS and A level. Teachers of vocational subjects often have other backgrounds – for instance, a teacher of music technology may have experience as a recording engineer (though a formal teaching qualification is usually necessary). At university level, lecturers will need a further degree (usually a doctorate) and have an interest in academic research, though formal teaching qualifications are rarely required at this level.

Key points

- There are lots of ways to achieve a fulfilling and lucrative career through music.
- You cannot choose a career in music for your child, but you can be aware of the possibilities and give advice, guidance and encouragement when requested.
- Encourage your child to be flexible and adaptable when aiming for a career in music.
- There are many different paths to a career in music; don't worry if it takes your child time to find one.
- Even though music career structures are often informal, there is no substitute for gaining relevant qualifications and experience.

USEFUL WORDS

Musicians, like all specialists, have developed their own ways of speaking to describe what they do. While this is useful for people who understand it, it can be difficult for anyone who does not. The list below is not a music dictionary, but it explains the musical terms used in this book, as well as some everyday words which have a specific musical meaning.

(Words which refer to specific instruments are only included if they appear in the book, so if you come across other words referring to instruments that you don't understand, it may be useful to look at your child's tutor book or the instrument manual, or talk to the teacher.)

If your child, or your child's teacher, uses a musical term you don't know, it may help to look for it in this list so that you have a basic idea of what it means. But remember that it is often useful to ask for an explanation too. If your child uses an unfamiliar musical word or phrase, ask what it means. If children find it easy to explain something, it is an indication that they understand it well themselves. You can also show your interest by asking your child's teacher about things you don't understand. (Bear in mind too that many technical words mean different things to different teachers – you may need to ask for clarification if you feel you need to understand something in detail.)

Any word shown in *italic* type in the text has its own entry in the list.

absolute pitch the ability to identify and name any *pitch* when hearing it in isolation (also known as 'perfect pitch'). Many musicians with absolute pitch can sing any pitch on demand – when asked to sing F sharp, for example, they will reproduce the pitch without needing to hear it on an instrument first, and it will be in tune when checked against an independent reference. For many years it was thought that absolute pitch was a facility that certain people were born with; research now suggests that it can be learned and developed like any other musical skill.

Absolute pitch can help many aspects of music-making – memorization, imitation, identification of pitch and *intervals*, and *improvisation* – though some people with absolute pitch find it difficult to *transpose* or play a *transposing instrument.*

accent a type of *articulation* mark

accompaniment any musical *part* that is played at the same time as the main part. For example, a piece for flute may have a piano accompaniment, or a church choir may be accompanied by an organ. See also *solo.*

acoustic word used to describe any musical instrument that does not need electricity or amplification to be heard (for example, acoustic guitar). See also *acoustics*.

acoustics the science of sound and how it works. Musicians refer to the acoustics (or acoustic) of a room or concert hall when talking about its qualities for making music – how the sound moves around, whether the performers and audience can hear clearly, the amount of echo and so on.

amplifier an electric or electronic device used to make the sound of an instrument louder. Some instruments (e.g. certain electronic keyboards) make no noise at all without an amplifier. Others (including the human voice) sound without amplification but are sometimes amplified to make their sound louder (in large halls, for example, or where many other instruments are playing).

arpeggio the notes of a *chord* played one after the other. On many instruments, learning arpeggios in different *keys* is an important way of developing *technique*.

arrangement a version of a tune or piece made for a different instrument or group of instruments. For example, a tune that was first written for trumpet can be published as a new arrangement for flute; or a piece originally written to be played by many people in an orchestra can be arranged for one person to play on the piano (this is known as a *reduction*). Arrangements can also be simplified versions of pieces.

articulation the way in which individual notes are joined together by the player to make musical sense. Marks in the music tell musicians to join or separate notes in different ways. For example, curved lines above or below notes (slurs) mean that the notes must be played 'legato' – joined smoothly from one to the next. Notes with dots above or below them are to be played 'staccato' – short and separated from each other. The articulation sign > above or below a note is an accent – an instruction to play the note more forcefully than the ones around it.

audition a performance given by a musician to demonstrate his or her abilities as part of an application to join an orchestra or band, gain entry to a school or music college, etc. The format of an audition will vary: sometimes the candidate can choose what music to play; sometimes there are set pieces or tasks.

aural tests the section of a music exam which is intended to assess the candidate's listening skills or *ear*. Tests may involve singing, clapping, playing, beating time or conducting, as well as commenting on various aspects of

167

music played by the examiner. The best preparation for aural tests is regular *ear-training*.

bar a unit of musical time. A bar is a group of *beats*. The *time signature* shows the number of beats in a bar, which varies from piece to piece and sometimes within a piece too. In printed music, the divisions between bars are shown by vertical lines (bar-lines).

beat a single instance of a *pulse*. Just as a single heartbeat is one isolated event within the body's continuous, regular pulse, so a beat is a single unit of time within the pulse that underlies a piece of music. Beats are grouped together (most usually in twos, threes or fours) to form *bars*. 'Beat' is also used more generally to mean the same as pulse or *rhythm* – the propulsive energy that drives the music along; and it is also the word for the gestures a conductor makes to show the *time signature* and *tempo* of the music.

body percussion see *percussion*

bow hold the position of the hand and fingers needed when holding the bow of a *string instrument*

bowing the alternation of pulling and pushing the bow across the strings. Bowing marks above the notes tell the player of a *string instrument* in which direction to move the bow. Bowing is also a form of *articulation* as it governs the way notes are linked together or separated from each other.

168

brass instruments *wind instruments* that are usually made from brass or another metal; the sound is made by the vibration of the player's lips against the mouthpiece.

broken chord see *arpeggio*

chamber music music performed by small groups of players, normally without a conductor

chord two or more notes played or sung together. Chords are played on a keyboard by pressing several keys at once, and on a guitar or harp by plucking several strings at the same time. In a choir or *orchestra*, chords are created by different voices or instruments singing or playing notes together.

concert pitch the *pitch* at which an instrument actually sounds. The piano and most string instruments are played at concert pitch so the written notes match the sounds they make. A *transposing instrument* is one where concert pitch and written pitch do not match. The term is also used to mean a reference *tuning* (usually A=440Hz) used by orchestral instruments so that they are all in tune with each other.

conductor the person who directs a choir, *orchestra* or other large group of musicians. The conductor normally stands in front of the musicians and directs the *tempo*, *dynamics* and *interpretation* of the music.

conservatoire (or conservatory) a music college where musicians can study at higher education level after leaving school. Some conservatoires have junior departments for younger pupils.

director see *music director*

dynamics how loud or quiet music is performed, and changes in levels of volume within a piece; also the marks in written music which tell the performer how loudly or quietly to play

ear the ability to hear and understand music when playing or listening. A musician with a good ear is one who can easily detect (and reproduce by singing or playing) musical details such as *pulse*, *rhythm*, *pitch* and *intervals*. A pupil's musical ear is developed by *ear-training* and assessed in music exams by *aural tests*.

ear-training exercises and tests which develop the musical *ear*. In the early stages of learning, teachers often introduce ear-training through a range of games involving listening, playing, singing and clapping. As the ear improves, teachers use a variety of activities to stimulate and train it; ideally this process should continue throughout a musician's career.

169

embouchure the position of the lips, teeth, tongue and jaw when playing a *woodwind* or *brass instrument*

ensemble any small- to medium-sized group of players or singers, made up of any combination of instruments and/or voices. Some standard groups exist, particularly for classical *chamber music*. The word is also used when describing how well any group of musicians plays together ('ensemble' is French for 'together'); a festival or competition judge may praise the 'ensemble' of a group, meaning that its members play particularly well in time and in tune with each other.

expression the details of a musical performance which go beyond the mechanical reproduction of the notes themselves. These include *dynamics*, *articulation*, *phrasing* and *vibrato*, all of which contribute to the *interpretation* of a piece of music. Instructions in printed music which direct the player to perform in a particular way are often known as expression marks.

fingering the placing of the fingers on a musical instrument. On nearly all instruments (apart from the trombone and most *percussion* instruments), each *pitch* or *chord* is produced by using a different position or a different combination of fingers on the keys, strings or holes. (On some *woodwind* and *brass instruments* different pitches are produced from the same fingering by being blown differently.) In order to move fluently from one note or chord to the next, players need to practise fingering until it becomes almost automatic. In written music (for *keyboard* and *string instruments* in particular), 'fingering' also refers to small numbers written above or below the notes; these advise the player which finger might best be used for which note.

harmony two or more different *pitches* sounding simultaneously; also the way in which *chords* are constructed and fit together, and the way they fit to a *melody*. Adding a chordal *accompaniment* to a tune – known as harmonization – is frequently tested in *theory* and *musicianship* tests.

improvising/improvisation creating music (singing or playing) spontaneously, without preparation or planning. Improvisation does not rely on printed music; instead it uses a particular musical feature as a starting point – such as a series of *chords* or a *rhythm* – which the performers develop as they wish. Improvisation is important for all musicians, and is particularly used in jazz, pop and rock music. A good teacher will encourage pupils to improvise as part of their training, and the ability to improvise is often examined in *aural* and *musicianship* tests.

170

interpretation the way in which a musician or group performs a piece of music, turning it from *notation* (or idea) into something that can be heard and experienced by an audience. Printed music gives the performer many instructions – for example, what notes to play, how loudly or quietly, and how quickly or slowly – but individual performers interpret these instructions in different ways, which means that no two performances of the same piece will sound identical. The choices that a musician makes give each performance (and each performer) a different character. A competition judge may praise a candidate's interpretation, meaning that he or she gave a convincing, musical performance with real character and individuality.

interval the distance between any two *pitches*. Intervals are measured by the number of steps between pitches, and have names that reflect these numbers (e.g. '6th' and '7th'). An *octave* is a specific type of interval.

intonation accuracy of *pitch* or *tuning*. On some instruments, the player has direct control over the pitch. These include voice, many *woodwind* and *brass instruments* and unfretted *string instruments*. There are many ways in which a player can affect the pitch – these include finger position, *bow hold*, amount of breath, and shape of *embouchure*. 'Good intonation' is when all the notes the player produces are accurately pitched in relation to each other, and in relation to those produced by other instruments around them. One purpose of *ear-training* is to help pupils with intonation.

Some aspects of intonation cannot be directly controlled by the player. For instance, a piano may need *tuning*: if the strings are poorly adjusted this cannot be affected by the way a player presses the keys. String instruments (guitars in particular) may be poorly set up and impossible to play in tune; on woodwind and brass instruments problems with keys, holes and valves can seriously affect intonation (see *set-up*).

key the *scale* and *chords* that form the basis of a particular piece of music. Most western European and American music uses 24 different keys. These are identified by letter names, in various combinations with the words sharp, flat, major and minor. A piece based on the scale and chords of A flat major is described as being 'in the key of A flat major' – this usually means that it will start and finish on the note or chord of A flat. Other musical traditions have different systems of keys and other ways of describing music (see also *mode*), and some music uses no key system at all.

keyboard instruments any instrument that is played using a keyboard. Each key controls a different pitch. The sound may be produced in many different ways depending on the specific instrument – on a piano the keys control hammers which hit strings, on an electronic keyboard the sound is produced electronically, and on a pipe organ the keys control a mechanism which allows air to be blown into pipes.

171

legato see *articulation*

masterclass a lesson given to a group of students by a famous musician

measure another word for *bar*. It is an American term but is frequently used in the UK as well.

melody a coherent sequence of individual musical sounds, one after the other – often described as a tune. Melodies are usually made up of different *notes* and *intervals*. They vary in length and complexity. 'Melody' is also used to refer to the *solo* line in a piece with several *parts*, to distinguish it from the *accompaniment*.

metronome a mechanical or electronic device for setting a *pulse*. The pulse can be marked by clockwork or electronic ticks, a flashing light or even a digitally recorded voice. The metronome can be adjusted to regulate the number of *beats* per minute; some metronomes also indicate the first beat of each *bar* (the length of the bar is adjusted by the user). A metronome can be used as an indicator of *tempo* – composers often put a metronome mark at the start of a piece of music to show how quickly or slowly it should be played. Some teachers encourage pupils to practise (particularly *scales* and *arpeggios*) against a metronome to develop regular, even playing.

MIDI [Musical Instrument Digital Interface] a system that enables computers to control electronic musical instruments and sound modules, and electronic instruments to connect to and control one another. A MIDI file is a set of data which gives instructions to a computer or electronic instrument, specifying the details (among them *pitch*, volume, duration and instrumentation) of how sounds should be reproduced during playback.

mixing balancing the individual musical instruments or sound sources when recording, DJing or sound engineering at a live performance

mode a sequence of *pitches* that moves by step. Modes differ from standard major or minor *scales* because they have different patterns of *intervals*. But like scales, modes form the basis of a wide variety of music and are the building-blocks of *melody* and *harmony* in a lot of jazz, traditional and world music.

music director the person who directs a choir, orchestra or other group. A music director will usually be a *conductor* but is likely also to select *repertoire* and plan the activities of the group; an educational function may also be involved. In theatre work, he or she is also likely to make *arrangements* of the music for performance by a specific collection of musicians.

musicianship the range of abilities a musician needs besides instrumental or vocal *technique*. The basic skills include an ability to read music from *notation* and understand what it means; a good understanding of music *theory* and how it affects practical music-making; accurate *sight-reading*; a well-developed *ear*; good *intonation*, *timing* and musical memory. Beyond this, opinions vary – but most teachers would agree that important aspects of musicianship include an understanding of *interpretation* and of how to make music expressive. A number of boards run exams in musicianship – these are likely to test the skills listed above, as well as the candidate's ability to *improvise*, *transpose*, add *harmony* to a *melody*, and create *accompaniments* and *arrangements*.

music service an organization in the UK contracted by a local education authority to provide music tuition in state schools and at music centres

music technology the application of electronics and computing to the creation, performance and capture of music. This usually means the use of keyboards and other electronic instruments, computers (together with relevant software) and recording equipment for music-making and music education. See also *sequencing*.

notation any means of writing music down so that it can be read and repro-duced at a later stage. Standard music notation – the lines, dots and symbols found in printed music – is just one way of doing this. Many musicians work from other systems: rock guitarists favour tab (short for 'tablature'), which shows the position of the fingers on the frets; drummers also have a specific notation suited to their needs. Other musicians – particularly in folk, rock and pop traditions – do not use standard notation, relying on home-made notation systems to capture and transmit their work (but more often they do this through audio recording).

In education, young children are often encouraged to explore different ways of notating sounds and exchanging musical ideas. However, standard notation has remained largely unchanged and unchallenged for hundreds of years because it is relatively easy to learn, flexible and an ideal way of enabling musicians to read and reproduce the work of others.

note a unit of musical sound. Most people use the word to describe any pitched sound (see *pitch*) made by a voice or instrument. Many teachers and musicians apply a stricter definition and only use the word 'note' for a musical sound that has both pitch and duration. Music *notation* specifies (among other things) both of these measurements – how high or low and how long and short each note should be.

octave the name given to the *interval* between any *pitch* and the next pitch of the same name above or below it

orchestra a large group of musicians, usually (but not always) playing classical music

part an individual line of music. Very little music, in whatever style, is just one unaccompanied line – most of it is created by a number of musicians playing different parts together (or, in the case of a *solo* piano or guitar, for example, by the performer playing several notes at once). For some types of music, each part is taken by one player – a string quartet, for example, has four musicians, each playing one part. For others, each part is taken by several musicians. In a choir, for instance, each part is sung by several singers and there may also be an *accompaniment* (piano, organ or *orchestra*).

percussion instruments which are sounded by being struck, shaken, rubbed or scraped – drums, bells, rattles, woodblocks and so on. (Strictly, a piano is a percussion instrument because when the keys are pressed, hammers hit the strings.) 'Tuned percussion' refers to struck instruments that make *pitched* sounds, such as the xylophone or timpani. Some teachers use the phrase 'body percussion' to describe noises made with the body, such as hand-claps, foot-stamps, and finger- and tongue-clicks.

perfect pitch see *absolute pitch*

phrase/phrasing a short sequence of individual musical sounds. A phrase is a self-contained unit of notes within a *melody*. Understanding the phrases or phrasing in a piece of music – knowing where they begin and end, and expressing this in performance – is rather like understanding the grammar and punctuation in text, and is an important part of *interpretation*.

pitch the measurement of how high or low a musical sound is. A child's voice tends to be higher in pitch than an adult's. Usually, on a *string instrument*, the thicker the string, the lower the pitch. In music, pitches are named after the first seven letters of the alphabet.

Some musicians use the word pitch to refer to *intonation*, and talk about 'pitching' a note – getting it exactly in tune. Most musical instruments make 'pitched' sounds (sounds that can be measured as physical frequencies and named) but some, like cymbals and some other *percussion* instruments, make unpitched sounds.

pulse a constant, regular repetition of a sound, movement, signal or sensation. In music, the pulse helps musicians to play in time with each other and, by counting each *beat* of the pulse, to measure the length of individual notes. The speed of the pulse – the rate at which the beats repeat – governs the speed or *tempo* of a piece of music.

174

range the distance between the lowest and highest *pitches* of a musical instrument (or individual voice – this is often known as 'vocal range'). A piano, for example, has a greater range than a recorder.

reduction a type of *arrangement*

register a particular region of *pitches*. The word is used often to describe 'areas' of a particular voice or instrument where the sounds produced have a similar character and *timbre*. On a voice or instrument with a wide *range*, there may be a number of different registers.

relative pitch the ability to identify one *pitch* in relation to another. At its simplest, this is the ability to know whether one note is higher than another. *Ear-training* gradually helps musicians to refine this skill until they can understand (and often describe in detail) the distances between notes (see *interval*) and reproduce these quickly (and often subconsciously).

repertoire a stock or collection of music. The word can be used in several ways. The 'flute repertoire' means all the music composed for that instrument. Repertoire also designates all the pieces that a particular musician (or group of musicians) knows and is able to play. Acquiring a 'good repertoire' – a range of pieces in a variety of styles suitable for different occasions – is an important part of a musician's development.

rhythm a pattern of sounds of varying length. While a *pulse* is a steady, unchanging repetition of individual *beats*, a rhythm may contain notes of several different lengths. In a broader sense, rhythm also refers to the aspect of music relating to time (or what is left if you take away those aspects relating to *pitch* and *dynamic*).

scale a sequence of *pitches* that moves by step, upwards or downwards. There are several different types of scale. The most common are major, minor and chromatic. Each type follows a specific pattern of *intervals*. Scales of one type or another are the building-blocks of nearly all music. Whether playing or singing, musicians learn and practise scales from the earliest stages to the most advanced levels because they are one of the foundations of good *technique*.

score the complete printed *notation* for a piece of music, showing the *parts* for each instrument. 'Scoring' means writing or making an *arrangement* for *orchestra* or other *ensemble* – if a piece of music is described as 'scored for wind quintet', for example, a full performance requires a flute, a clarinet, an oboe, a bassoon and a horn.

sequencing in *music technology*, a method of storing, recording and manipulating musical data, using *MIDI* or audio

set-up how an instrument is maintained and prepared for playing. All instruments need some form of attention to keep them in top condition, though some need more careful adjustment than others. For example, the bridge on a *string instrument* has to be at the correct height and in the correct position; the strings have to be in good condition; and the pegs have to turn smoothly but not too easily. On a *woodwind instrument*, all the keys and connecting rods must function perfectly; the pads that cover the holes need to be in good condition; the mouthpiece needs careful protection; and, where relevant, the reeds need proper preparation. Some aspects of an instrument's set-up can be handled at home by the pupil or parent, but many of them will need expert attention from the teacher or an instrument repairer.

sight-reading reading and playing a piece of printed music without having previously seen it or having had the opportunity to practise it. (Singers often refer to this skill as 'sight-singing'.) Any musician who uses printed music will need basic sight-reading skills. In a music exam, sight-reading is tested by giving the candidate a short piece to play or sing and allowing him or her a short amount of time to scan the music before performing it. Sight-reading is not confined to standard printed music – jazz and pop musicians often need to sight-read chord charts and other forms of *notation*. Sight-reading skills need to be developed by frequent practice.

solo a piece or passage of music performed by a single instrument or voice, with or without *accompaniment*. A piece described as 'for solo flute' is for one flute player, without accompaniment; but 'solo flute repertoire' might refer to a range of pieces both with and without accompaniment in which the flute is given the most prominent part. In the context of an *orchestra* or band, a solo is usually a section of a larger piece in which one player's *part* is the centre of attention while the rest of the musicians provide an accompaniment or are silent. In jazz, a solo is usually an opportunity for an individual musician to display his or her *improvisation* skills over the backing of the rest of the band.

staccato see *articulation*

string instruments instruments whose sound is produced by vibrating strings mounted on a wooden box. The strings can be made to vibrate by means of plucking (a guitar, for instance) or by the use of a bow (a violin or cello, for example).

study a piece of music written specifically to develop *technique*

syllabus the list of requirements for an exam, competition or festival

technique the mechanical aspects of singing, or playing an instrument. The study of technique covers the physical and psychological aspects of how the sound is produced, controlled and modified. Technique is usually developed by frequent practice, particularly of *scales, arpeggios* and *studies.*

tempo the speed of a piece of music. Tempo is governed by the speed of the *pulse* – the faster the pulse, the faster the tempo. At the beginning of a piece of music, a composer may show the desired tempo by means of a *metronome* marking, indicating the number and type of *beats* per minute. Another method is to use written tempo indications – words (often in Italian) which describe how quickly or slowly the music should be played.

theory the study of how music works, how it is written down and how it is created. Music theory exams test a candidate's ability to understand the rules of *notation, melody, harmony* and *rhythm*. A student of music theory may also need to have some knowledge of musical instruments and their characteristics and to be able to identify different styles of music and the work of various composers.

timbre the sound quality of a voice or instrument, sometimes referred to as its tone. Many different factors affect the timbre of an instrument – its *acoustics* are governed by the way it is constructed and the materials it is made from, as well as other considerations like its age, its *set-up* or state of repair, and the temperature and humidity of the room in which it is played. The way it is played is also a factor – a skilled musician can often coax a good tone from even the poorest instrument. Singers are trained to improve the timbre and power of their voice by controlling the muscles that affect vocal production.

time signature the numbers that appear vertically above one another at the start of a piece of music (and sometimes during a piece too). The upper figure refers to the number of *beats* in each *bar*, and the lower figure to the rhythmic value of each beat.

timing accuracy of *rhythm*, usually against a *pulse*. A musician with a good sense of timing is able to fit notes to a pulse and to maintain a steady rhythm without getting faster or slower. Individual musicians within a group need a good sense of timing in order to create a good *ensemble*. Some teachers use the word 'timing' when referring to a *time signature*.

tone (1) the sound quality of a voice or instrument – see *timbre*; (2) a specific type of *interval* which is also known as a whole tone or major 2nd; (3) another word for *pitch* – meaning a musical sound without specified duration; (4) another word (often used in the USA) for *note*. Many musicians use interchangeably meanings 3 and 4.

transpose to move music out of one *key* into another. For example, a singer may find a piece of written music too high or low for his or her *range*. In order for the song to be sung comfortably, it will need to be transposed (moved higher or lower) – as will any *accompaniment*. This can either be done in advance (writing out the music in the new key) or – if the performers are sufficiently able – on the fly while playing. While the ability to transpose is more necessary on some instruments than others, it is an important part of general *musicianship*.

177

transposing instruments instruments which, when they are played, make sounds that are higher or lower than the written note. For various reasons, many *woodwind* and *brass instruments*, and some *string instruments* (such as double bass and guitar) are written at one *pitch* and sound at another. This means, for example, that the written note C played on a clarinet will not sound at the same pitch as the note C on a piano. Printed music is normally 'pre-transposed' so that all the *parts* sound correct together.

tuning adjusting an instrument to make it play at the correct *pitch*. Most instruments that are assembled or prepared for playing by the user need to be tuned. This involves making sure that the instrument is playing at the correct pitch by checking it against a fixed instrument (such as a piano or keyboard) or a tuning device (such as a *tuning fork* or electronic tuner); or against another instrument that has already been tuned. (In an orchestra, most players tune to the pitch of the note A on the oboe, which the oboist will have already tuned independently.)

The method of adjustment depends on the type of instrument. *String instruments* are adjusted by turning the pegs to increase tension in the strings (which raises the pitch) or reduce tension (which lowers the pitch). To adjust a *wind instrument*, the player needs to alter the length of the tube in some way – usually by adjusting the position of the mouthpiece. Lengthening the tube lowers the pitch; shortening it raises the pitch. The word tuning is also used to refer to *intonation*.

tuning fork a small u-shaped metal fork with two prongs. When struck gently, the fork produces a specific *pitch* which can then be used as a reference when *tuning* an instrument. The most common tuning fork is the *concert pitch* A (440Hz), which is the standard tuning note for most orchestral instruments.

unpitched see *pitch*

vibrato a musical effect where the *pitch* of a note is quickly raised and lowered by a very small amount. This adds warmth and expressiveness to the music. It is possible on all instruments that allow the player direct control over the pitch, and this includes the voice.

vocal cords the muscles in the throat that produce sound when we speak or sing. Most singing teachers prefer the term 'vocal folds', which more accurately reflects the shape of the muscle.

warm-ups exercises used by musicians to prepare for performing or practising. By warming up gently before they play, singers and instrumentalists avoid damage to their muscles.

wind instruments instruments that are sounded by being blown. Most wind instruments fall into one of two categories: woodwind (see *woodwind instruments*) or brass (see *brass instruments*). Pipe organs and accordions might also technically be described as wind instruments since sound is made by having air blown into the instrument, but they are most usually described as *keyboard instruments*.

woodwind instruments category of instruments comprising flutes, recorders and reed instruments that are sounded by the player blowing air into them; traditionally made from wood, they can also be made out of metal (flutes and saxophones) or plastic (clarinets and recorders).

INDEX

183

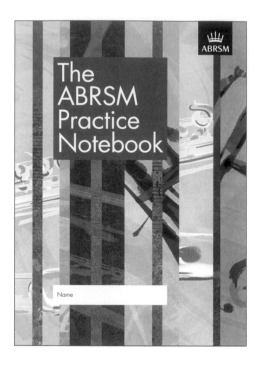

The ABRSM Practice Notebook

- filled with useful hints and advice on practising, a holiday practice diary and much more
- allows teachers to record their students' progress and set goals
- useful for parents when guiding their children's practice

ISBN 978-1-86096-930-0

First Steps in Music Theory
Eric Taylor

- a step-by-step presentation of the basic facts of music theory
- clear, easily understood explanations
- an excellent resource for anyone learning to read music
- ideal for students preparing for exams

ISBN 978-1-86096-090-1

Music Theory in Practice
Eric Taylor

- a clear explanation of music notation
- definitions of important words and concepts
- straightforward language throughout
- many worked examples and practice exercises
- specimen exam questions

The *Music Theory in Practice* series has helped more than one million musicians worldwide to learn about the notation and theory of music.

Grade 1   ISBN 978-1-86096-942-3
Grade 2   ISBN 978-1-86096-943-0
Grade 3   ISBN 978-1-86096-944-7
Grade 4   ISBN 978-1-86096-945-4
Grade 5   ISBN 978-1-86096-946-1

Available from all good music retailers and www.abrsm.org